Unlikely Righteousness: Unsung Heroes of Genesis

Life Lessons from the Bible

Tina Kowalski

Published by Tina Kowalski Books, 2016.

While every precaution has been taken in the preparation of this book, the publisher assumes no responsibility for errors or omissions, or for damages resulting from the use of the information contained herein.

UNLIKELY RIGHTEOUSNESS: UNSUNG HEROES OF GENESIS

First edition. July 2, 2016.

Copyright © 2016 Tina Kowalski.

ISBN: 979-8223383055

Written by Tina Kowalski.

Table of Contents

To my father Gerald Kowalski. Your faith lives on even though you are no longer with us.

Introduction:

Let me ask you a very personal question: who are your heroes? For some of you may find it easy to answer. Without conscious thought a name or face comes instantly to mind. Some of you may hesitate as you go through your mental list before deciding what to say.

Now a follow-up question: why do you admire them? Heroes have the ability to inspire us in ways that we don't even realise. The ultimate hero of course is Jesus Christ whose selfless service and example has given hope to every man, woman and child who will ever live. Many people have followed His example and have touched the lives of those around them for good. Others are just learning about Him and forging their own path to become like Him. Even those who have never heard of Him can unintentionally follow His example through their desire to treat others as they would like to be treated.

The Bible and other Holy Scriptures give many examples of the three main types of people that we meet in life:

- Heroes. People whose good deeds are spectacular enough that to this day they are still talked about. Others within this group were so consistent in doing the right thing that you almost forget about their weaknesses and failings while reading their story.

- Villains. These people are the ones who went beyond what is decent and did horrible things to at least one other person. In many cases they never tried to make amends and took pride in the devastation that they caused leaving us with a bad taste in our mouth, and a desire to never become like them, whenever we read or hear their names.

- Those people who are somewhere in between. They may have been good before making a horrible decision that they never quite recovered from or conversely, they may have started off pretty rough before making a life-changing decision that benefitted their lives forever. Other people in this group were consistently good but never did anything too noteworthy so have been fairly ignored by popular media for several centuries. Lastly, are the most relatable members of this group - those people who in our estimation had an even number of good and bad deeds.

Each of the three main groups listed above is interesting and worth studying in their own right, as they can all help us in our journey through life, but for the purposes of this book I would like to focus on those in group #3.

That's right, this book is dedicated to those people who I consider to be the unsung heroes of the Bible. Don't get me wrong David, Moses, Esther, Ruth, Joshua, Peter, James,

UNLIKELY RIGHTEOUSNESS: UNSUNG HEROES OF GENESIS

John, Paul, Noah and all the other well-known Biblical people deserve the fame that they have received. Each one of them teaches us how to have faith and overcome huge trials but they already have people talking about them, writing songs about them, and/or painting moments from their lives. Due to my battle with weight, intense shyness and social awkwardness, and convincing myself that the only thing that I had going for me was my intellect I know what it is like to feel like you aren't getting the recognition you crave. I have no idea if these people are upset by the fact that many people don't know who they are (I got several blank and confused looks when I talked to family and friends about some of them while writing this book) but my goal is to identify those whose faith and actions should be significant to us and to give them their moment in the sun. Some of their stories end with them continuing to live the gospel while sadly others started off well but somewhere along the way they chose the wrong path and are known more for their mistakes than their successes. Some of them are key members of the story but for some reason have never been considered significant enough for their names to be known. In addition to their ability to instruct us on how to behave the people in this book offer us another benefit - they show us how much God loves each of his children regardless of race, gender, or religion.

Another reason that some of these people may not be very well known is that their righteousness catches us off guard and surprises us. Many of these people fall into three main groups. These people were either:

- from a nation where we would not expect them to

have heard of the Lord's commandments, to be following them, or be receptive to them and yet are;

- they may have been viewed as "bad people" because their best-known actions were not what God wanted and led to serious consequences for themselves or others. I've included this group of people because at one time in their lives they did show a certain amount of righteousness either before or after their notorious actions and that should be acknowledged; and/or

- people who were obedient to the commandments and did not use their circumstances to justify breaking them. This group of people showed great courage and is especially important to those of us living in the modern age as they show us the importance of obedience no matter what life throws at us.

I consider all of these people to be interesting but do not claim to have a perfect understanding of their motivations and reasons for doing what they did. Even scholars cannot say with 100% certainty that they know all of the motivations of the people they study because one of the biggest challenges we face when writing their stories is that the Bible is **irritatingly silent** at times. Many of the details and tools that you would use today to write a biography are simply not available.

UNLIKELY RIGHTEOUSNESS: UNSUNG HEROES OF GENESIS

One of the challenges that I faced when writing this book is that I cannot interview them, or someone that knew them, and ask clarifying questions because they have all been dead for millennia. I also don't know how much the prevailing culture of their day affected their behaviour so can't say with certainty "they [insert behaviour or statement here] because of [insert cultural belief, custom, or tradition]". For example, Abraham was monotheistic during a time when most people believed in multiple gods. His behaviour would be considered "weird" for his day and yet we never question it because it is fairly normal for ours. The last issue I faced when writing their stories is that there are blanks in the text as the writers were selective in who they focused on causing us to lose track of the other people we have been following for several years before we meet them again or we may never hear their name again except in the genealogies.

Although these things were frustrating, they gave me the opportunity to do my own detective work to come up with logical conclusion. I tried to ask questions and visualise the situation from multiple angles so that I could try to empathise with the person and those around them.

As a Latter-Day Saint, I also used quotes from modern day apostles and prophets, study manuals, and other resources where available to try and get insight where there are blanks in the text.

When necessary, I used my own personal experiences with other people and/or the experiences of others that I've known to try and fill in the blanks. For example, while not a mother myself I have known several mothers so I can use the information I've gleaned from them to try and get inside the heads of the women in this book who were mothers.

Lastly, I considered what information they may have had available at each point in their story and gave them the benefit of the doubt when a lack of information may have influenced their decisions. I tried to always remember that they were human and made just as many mistakes as I do/will, that they did not know exactly how their future was going to pan out even when they received revelation from God, and that they may have had their own spiritual/emotional wounds that affected their decisions that we just don't know about.

As with all stories I have tried to identify at least one thing these people can teach us. Call them the "moral of the story" if you will but at the end of each chapter there are one to three lessons that we can learn from these stories. This is not a comprehensive list however and, based on your experience and perspective, you may be able to identify lessons from these people's lives as well. I hope so because that will help you to get to know them better yourself.

I hope that you enjoy this book and that you use this as an opportunity to make some new spiritual friends. Each of these people is still spiritually alive and I hope you too look forward to meeting them one day just as I do. I would also invite you to go one step further and as you read their stories think about the times you may or may not have been aware of God's hand in your life. You may be surprised as you recall all the times he has said "I love you" to you throughout your life.

Cain - Good Guy
Gone Bad

Cain is the first "Bad Boy" in history and for good reason - he killed his brother and then tried to get away with it. The story of Cain is a tragedy because we will never know WHAT he could have accomplished if he had not made the choices that lead him to become the first murderer in history. As I've read about Cain, I've come to the conclusion that he once was a decent man, although always slightly rebellious[1], whose choices lead him to where he ultimately ended up. I would also suspect that if we could ask him if it was worth it, he would probably say no. How do I know this? Well let's look at his story and where he ended up.

Cain was the first named son[2] of Adam and Eve, our first parents. He is described to us as being a tiller of the ground while his brother Abel raised flocks. Like many of the people found in the scriptures many of the details of his life are missing from the account, including the exact relationships he had with his parents and siblings, however we can learn a bit about him by examining his chosen occupation. Growing crops takes time, patience and optimism because you are gambling for things to work out exactly the way you need them to so that you can feed your family and community. If anything goes wrong you either have a reduced harvest or no harvest at all which could lead to starvation or poverty. It takes hard work, determination, knowledge of the best conditions for growth, and other skills that can often take a lifetime to develop. I have watched several farmers and know that this is not a career choice for those who are faint of heart so we can assume that Cain bravely hoped for a successful harvest year after year.

Now let's look at the other main character in this story: Abel. Raising flocks contains its own challenges such as finding adequate feed, protecting them from predation, and ensuring that your flock grows larger and healthier every year making it just as hard an occupation as Cain's but in a different way. While they chose different "career" paths I would hope that the brothers shared a mutual respect for each other given that they both had the same desire to provide for their family and community. Let's hope that they didn't engage in the juvenile game of "my job is harder than your job" that some people play today.

Besides knowing that the two brothers had different occupations the Bible also tells us that they had different attitudes when it came to obeying the commandments of the Lord. This is shown by their choice in the sacrifices they offered and the Lord's reactions to them.

"And in process of time it came to pass, that Cain brought of the fruit of the ground an offering unto the Lord. And Abel, he also brought of the firstlings of his flock and of the fat thereof. And the Lord had respect unto Abel and to his offering: But unto Cain and to his offering he had not respect. And Cain was very wroth, and his countenance fell."[3]

UNLIKELY RIGHTEOUSNESS: UNSUNG HEROES OF GENESIS

Cain's sacrifice was rejected and he was angry. In this case he should have directed his anger towards himself because he knew better. God had left specific instructions on how the sacrifices were to be done and Cain ignored them. He also didn't offer the sacrifice for the right reasons. Animal sacrifices represented the upcoming death of Jesus Christ and so were prescribed to be done in a very specific manner in order to show that the person understood the symbolism, looked forward to the day when Christ would come in the flesh, and was willing to be exactly obedient.[4] Adam and Eve would have taught this to their children so we can assume that Cain knew this and that his offering of an inappropriate sacrifice was a deliberate act of disobedience and also a sign of laziness as he could have obtained an animal to sacrifice but chose not to.[5] Heavenly Father was disappointed in Cain for his disobedience but He loved Cain enough to want to help him in his progression. We know this because like any good father He took him aside, gave him some warnings, and explained what he needed to do to get it right.

"And the Lord said unto Cain, Why art thou wroth? and why is thy countenance fallen? If thou doest well, shalt thou not be accepted? and if thou doest not well, sin lieth at the door. And unto thee shall be his desire, and thou shalt rule over him."[6]

Modern revelation gives us a few more details from their conversation and also shows that other people wanted Cain to succeed as well and were trying to help him but **he didn't want their help**.

"And the Lord said unto Cain: Why art thou wroth? Why is thy countenance fallen? **If thou doest well, thou shalt be accepted**. And if thou doest not well, sin lieth at the door, **and Satan desireth to have thee; and except thou shalt hearken unto my commandments, I will deliver thee up**, and it shall be unto thee according to his desire. And thou shalt rule over him; **For from this time forth thou shalt be the father of his lies; thou shalt be called Perdition; for thou wast also before the world. And it shall be said in time to come—That these abominations were had from Cain; for he rejected the greater counsel which was had from God; and <u>this is a cursing which I will put upon thee, except thou repent</u>. And Cain was wroth, and listened not any more to the voice of the Lord, neither to Abel, his brother, who walked in holiness before the Lord.**"[7]

Now when I read the above accounts, I see something very significant to our understanding of not only Cain but also of God - **Cain was not surprised or afraid by the fact that God was talking to him!** Other men found in the scriptures, such as Moses, Samuel, and Saul/Paul, who later became great leaders, were surprised, fearful or confused when their initial conversation with God or one of His heavenly messengers occurred. Instead of being any of these things Cain becomes angry and exhibits a "you can't tell me what to do" attitude towards God and his family. This can only lead me to conclude one thing - this was not the first conversation that he'd had with God throughout his life. Perhaps it was the fact that God did talk to him regularly that made it easier for Cain to eventually ignore him. Sadly, we may never know how long God came to him and patiently gave him instructions and warnings designed to make him happy and keep him from making a fatal mistake. We don't know how many times Abel, Adam, Eve and/or his other relatives may have tried to stop him from going down a road they could see would eventually lead to his going off a spiritual cliff.[8] The conversation he had with God here shows that Cain could still have turned around and repented - at this point he had not passed the point of no return. Sadly, all of the warnings and instructions were in vain because like a rebellious teenager who thinks he knows everything Cain had gotten to the point where his attitude had become "Leave me alone. I'm a big boy and I can do what I like" and he decided to get rid of one of the messengers.

"And Cain talked with Abel his brother: and it came to pass, when they were in the field, that Cain rose up against Abel his brother, and slew him."[9]

I have both a sister and a brother. I have used the phrase "I'm going to kill you" at least a few times in the past when I have been particularly angry with them although I doubt that I would ever go through with it. As a sibling myself the brevity of this account leads me to come up with several questions such as:

- Did Abel suspect anything when Cain came and talked to him?
- Did Cain hesitate or was it easy for him to take another person's life?
- Did Abel have a chance to defend himself or did Cain take the cowardly approach and "stab him in the back" so to speak?
- Did anyone else know about this or were there no

witnesses or confidents to this altercation?

- What did Cain plan to tell others, especially his parents, when they asked him if he had seen Abel?

Modern revelation shows us that Cain plotted against his brother and that this was not a crime of passion.[10] Regardless of the circumstances surrounding Abel's death his murder was Cain's point of no return for two reasons:

1. He had taken into his own hands the right that only God has to decide when someone's life is over; and
2. He rejected the opportunity to be a man and repent when he was caught because he showed no remorse and failed to own up to what he had done.

"And the Lord said unto Cain, Where is Abel thy brother? And [Cain] said, I know not: Am I my brother's keeper?"[11]

The question "am I my brother's keeper" has become one of the most iconic phrases in history. According to one source this is what Cain implied with that phrase and it explains God's response to it:

"Sometimes this scripture is cited as evidence that each individual has a responsibility to love and care for his fellow men. Without question that responsibility is taught in the scriptures, but is that what Cain's question really implies? The Hebrew word which is translated as 'keeper' is *shomer* and means 'a guardian or custodian.' Thus, with typical Satanic deceitfulness, Cain's question twisted a true principle. No man has the right to be a keeper of his brethren in the sense of becoming their guard or custodian (except as assigned by civil law to guard criminals or in the case of parents and young children). And yet, for Cain to imply that he should have no concern for his fellowman, especially his literal brother, is to deny all gospel principles of love and concern for others."[12]

In addition to the callousness that the question "am I my brother's keeper" shows towards his fellow man this particular response shows one other thing about Cain - **he did not understand God**. If he had he would have realised that God already knew what had happened to Abel because He sees everything. Like his parents before him[13] the question God asked was not designed to find out information but to give Cain a chance to begin the repentance process by acknowledging his guilt, accepting responsibility, and learning about and accepting the consequences for the decision he had made. Cain didn't do that and so God was forced to play judge and dispense justice to Cain and for Abel.

"And [the Lord] said, What hast thou done? the voice of thy brother's blood crieth unto me from the ground. And now art thou cursed from the earth, which hath opened her mouth to receive thy brother's blood from thy hand; When thou tillest the ground, it shall not henceforth yield unto thee her strength; a fugitive and a vagabond shalt thou be in the earth."[14]

Thus far their conversation has been very short and to the point but it has also been useful for Cain because suddenly something clicks and he realises the seriousness of what he has done. Sadly, his response to God shows that there was still some remaining selfishness in him because there is no apology for what he did to Abel but instead a "woe is me" attitude and an acknowledgement that he does not want these consequences.

"And Cain said unto the Lord, My punishment is greater than I can bear. Behold, thou hast driven me out this day from the face of the earth; **and from thy face shall I be hid**; and I shall be a fugitive and a vagabond in the earth; and it shall come to pass, that every one that findeth me shall slay me."[15]

What were Cain's main concerns?

- He would be driven out of his community and essentially be homeless;
- He would no longer be able to converse with God; and
- He might also be murdered because of what he had done.

Once again God shows that He thought ahead because He already had a plan to allay one of these fears. As the father of all of us He didn't want any of His other children living then to follow in Cain's footsteps by murdering him so He implements a plan of protection.

UNLIKELY RIGHTEOUSNESS: UNSUNG HEROES OF GENESIS

"And the Lord said unto him, Therefore whosoever slayeth Cain, vengeance shall be taken on him sevenfold. And the Lord set a mark upon Cain, lest any finding him should kill him. **And Cain went out from the presence of the Lord**, and dwelt in the land of Nod, on the east of Eden."[16]

Let's recap the tragic consequences of Cain's most famous decision. An innocent man was killed, parents mourn for two of their sons, and a killer throws away the chance of a better life and to be an inspiration to those of us who are reading history instead of a warning. What a waste! Even with the horror that must have filled the heart of God having to deal with His son Cain for breaking such an important commandment still we see how much Heavenly Father loves us when He shows mercy to Cain. Although He will not be able to converse with Cain anymore, Heavenly Father prevents Cain from suffering an untimely death through the hands of His other children. Instead of leaving Cain in a vulnerable position where he may have suffered "mob justice" Heavenly Father put a mark on him to prevent other people from killing him. That is a sign of love and compassion.

In addition to losing contact with his Heavenly Father, and thereby ensuring that he would no longer be able to receive guidance from the source of all knowledge, Cain would have an unnecessarily difficult life in another way. One of the consequences of his actions resulted in him losing the ability to do what he loved most - help things grow. He would have to learn a new trade in order to support himself, which as a social outcast may have been difficult for him to do. How sad that Cain robbed himself of a better future in this way.

Morals of Cain's story:

1) Our limited vision can lead to heartache.

It should be no surprise to anyone reading this that seeing the future can sometimes be like looking into fog or murky water. As mortals we have a limited perspective and cannot always see where we are going to end up when we make decisions. In Cain's case he had some guides who tried to prevent him from falling off a spiritual cliff. Heavenly Father and Abel both came to Cain and tried to warn him because as outsiders they could see things that he couldn't. Instead of accepting their council and adjusting his course, he continued down a road that eventually led to murder, and a life that he **could not** really have wanted. May we not follow his example, and instead seek council from those who have our best interests at heart.

2) God is infinitely patient.

I truly believe from the text that Cain and Heavenly Father had several conversations besides the one that we have recorded. As these conversations were most likely deeply personal and sacred, we will never know some of the details such as what Cain was taught, how these conversations made him feel, and the good he did when he had listened to and followed the council given to him by Heavenly Father in the past. Heavenly Father is the perfect parent and He is unwilling to give up on us as long as there is even a particle of a chance that we can make it back to him. Even as Cain moved further and further away Heavenly Father still reached out and tried to help him. A wise person once said to me "God knows the difference between weakness and rebellion." If He was willing to continue helping someone who was deliberately rejecting Him, those of us who struggle with weaknesses can be comforted in knowing **He will never abandon us as long as we keep trying!**

3) **God will provide perfect justice.**

"Now it is better that a man should be judged of God than of man, for the judgments of God are always just, but the judgments of man are not always just."[17]

One of the greatest frustrations in this life for the victim(s) of a crime and their families is that our justice system is imperfect. Sometimes perpetrators go free or do not receive a full sentence for their crimes due to a lack of evidence, corruption of officials, no suspects, or other case specific factors. Although forensic science has made law enforcement's job easier it still cannot overcome all of these challenges.

Heavenly Father doesn't have any of these problems and is a man of His word. He has promised that in the end perfect justice will be served. He will not let the guilty get away with what they are doing nor will He allow the rewards of the righteous to be lost to them. While not all murderers, rapists, thieves, terrorists, and other criminals receive the perfect justice of God in this life, the story of Cain and Abel can give victims comfort in knowing that **God sees everything and justice will be served eventually**. Will that take away the pain experienced immediately - probably not - but it can provide some comfort because God will make it up to you. He is all powerful and is able to serve justice where others cannot. Also, the sacrifice of Jesus Christ has made it possible for us to be healed from all pain and heartache that we experience in this life. Abel was a righteous man. Even though Cain could take away his life he could not steal from him the blessings that he was entitled to because of the good things he did in his life. Abel would always be able to claim those and so will we be able to claim all blessings we are entitled to for our righteous decisions.

Pharaoh - Hobbies
Can Lead to
Heartache

One of the things that you notice when reading the Bible is how tied the children of Abraham are to Egypt. Although they interacted with all of the surrounding nations in one way or another Egypt just seems to be the place they are drawn to the most frequently. Often when the Israelites and the Egyptians interact, usually as a result of a famine or war, the leaders negotiated or otherwise influenced each other in both positive and negative ways.

"As long as there has been history, there has been Egypt. It is a country that bears witness of power that once was and of a power that will always be. Biblically, we often think of Egypt only in terms of the Old Testament. But Egypt's language and some of its people and customs form threads in the Book of Mormon[1] tapestry. It is the source behind much of the Pearl of Great Price. It is a land that has shaped empires and been shaped by them. It is a land that God has used for his purposes throughout all earthly time."[18]

---

1.   http://www.mormon.org/beliefs/book-of-mormon

Egyptian Pharaohs were great friends, hosts, helpers, and possibly even mentors of the patriarchs. Although we do not know what name to call the Pharaoh in Genesis 12, he has the distinct honour of meeting the first patriarch of the Israelite nation: Abram. Better known to us as Abraham, he comes to Egypt for the same reason that many of his descendants would - he was hungry.

"And there was a famine in the land: and Abram went down into Egypt to sojourn there; for the famine was grievous in the land."[19]

Famines were not an unusual thing in antiquity. Modern farming practices have not eliminated the risk of crop failure, they have simply reduced it. For the Bible to mention that the famine was "grievous" must have meant that it was abnormally bad. That would have made his life hard enough but Abram had another problem. His wife was so beautiful that other men were attracted to her to the point that, instead of just settling for admiring her from a distance, some men may have killed him so that they could possess her for themselves. Knowing that this was a possibility in Egypt Abram came up with a plan.

"And it came to pass, when he was come near to enter into Egypt, that he said unto Sarai his wife, Behold now, I know that thou art a fair woman to look upon: Therefore it shall come to pass, when the Egyptians shall see thee, that they shall say, This is his wife: and they will kill me, but they will save thee alive. Say, I pray thee, thou art my sister: that it may be well with me for thy sake; and my soul shall live because of thee."[20]

Tell everyone that you are single and my sister and then I won't be in danger. Good plan. Now like many people I don't agree with lying however modern revelation shows us that it wasn't completely Abram's idea.

"And it came to pass when I was come near to enter into Egypt, the Lord said unto me: Behold, Sarai, thy wife, is a very fair woman to look upon; Therefore it shall come to pass, when the Egyptians shall see her, they will say—She is his wife; and they will kill you, but they will save her alive; therefore see that ye do on this wise: Let her say unto the Egyptians, she is thy sister, and thy soul shall live. **And it came to pass that I, Abraham, told Sarai, my wife, all that the Lord had said unto me**—Therefore say unto them, I pray thee, thou art my sister, that it may be well with me for thy sake, and my soul shall live because of thee."[21]

OK now we have another problem: why would God ask one of his children to break one of the commandments that **He gave them** by telling half-truths? To understand you have to understand both God's character and His Plan of Salvation. This lie was necessary in order to protect Abram from customs of the day that God did not agree with (namely killing husbands to get their wives for yourself) and thus keep him alive until Abram was able to fulfill his role of starting the line through which the Saviour would come.

"And it came to pass, that, when Abram was come into Egypt, the Egyptians beheld the woman that she was very fair. The princes also of Pharaoh saw her, and commended her before Pharaoh: and the woman was taken into Pharaoh's house. And he entreated Abram well for her sake: and he had sheep, and oxen, and he asses, and menservants, and maidservants, and she asses, and camels."[22]

The word entreated means "to ask (a person) earnestly; beseech; beg"[23]. Based on that definition it sounds like Pharaoh was almost desperate to have her. As there are beautiful women in every country and culture this attests to the fact that Sarai must have been a very rare beauty even at an older age. It could also be noted that Pharaoh does show a degree of honour in that he doesn't just take her leaving Abram with nothing but compensates her "brother" for the loss of her help. Sadly, Pharaoh's lust and desperation led to new problems for him.

"And the Lord plagued Pharaoh and his house with great plagues because of Sarai Abram's wife."[24]

Now here is where we have to do a lot more speculation because many of the details are once again left out. For example, we don't know what the plagues were, how long they lasted, whether they were just within Pharaoh's household or across his entire nation, or what damage they did. What we can assume though is that they were out of the ordinary enough to get Pharaoh's attention and alert him that something was wrong. Another area that lacks detail from the text is how Pharaoh identified the source of his problems and how long it took him to figure out that Sarai and Abram had not been completely honest with him. Was it a dream from God? Did he just put two and two together that the issues had started after Sarai became a part of his household? Did one of his advisors help him figure it out? It doesn't say. All we know is that he did figure it out and that he wasn't happy with Abram when he confronted him about his lie.

"And Pharaoh called Abram, and said, What is this that thou hast done unto me? Why didst thou not tell me that she was thy wife? Why saidst thou, She is my sister? so I might have taken her to me to wife: now therefore behold thy wife, take her, and go thy way."[25]

For being somewhat brief we can conclude a few things from this little speech that help us learn about this Pharaoh's character.

- **Pharaoh respected marriage**.

We don't know how long she was in his household but his comment implies that he may have eventually married her instead of making her his mistress or concubine. It doesn't mention if he had talked to her or Abram about it yet so he may still have been making his mind up on the subject. Another thing to note is that he gives her back to her husband showing that he recognised who her authority figure really was and that spouses should not be separated.

- **Pharaoh was honest**.

This does not appear to be a hypocritical speech. Pharaoh would not have had a leg to stand on if he made a habit of lying so we can assume that he had been upfront with Abram from the beginning. We don't know what he was feeling when he confronted them - be it anger, confusion, hurt, exasperation, or some other emotion - but he does not appreciate that they lied to him leaving him open to potentially committing the crime of adultery by marrying an already married woman.

- **Pharaoh wanted them to leave.**

Pharaoh may have really liked and respected Abram. Only they and God truly know what their relationship was like. Regardless of any closeness in their relationship it is obvious that Abram had worn out his welcome. Whether Pharaoh was deeply hurt by their betrayal or just wanted to get the source of his problems away from him, Abram and Sarai were asked to leave Egypt. Pharaoh once again shows that he has a good character though by taking precautions to ensure that they would be safe while in his country. He warns his people to leave them alone.

"And Pharaoh commanded his men concerning [Abram]: and they sent him away, and his wife, and all that he had."[26]

It really is a shame that so many of the details of this story are left out because it limits our ability to entirely get to know this Pharaoh however there are a few things that we can learn from him from what we do have.

UNLIKELY RIGHTEOUSNESS: UNSUNG HEROES OF GENESIS

1) **When problems arise - look to see if you are responsible**.

There are three sources of the challenges that we face in life:

a) Challenges that are necessary in life. These include things like teething, growing pains, the joy that is puberty, and the common cold. While not often pleasant most people go through these challenges and we generally accept them as a part of life or rites of passage for us to transition from one life stage to another.

The other two sources of challenges come from choices and are optional.

b) Consequences from our own decisions and c) the consequences we receive due to the choices of others. As humans we often make mistakes or do things that are a bad idea. Examples include pouring gasoline on a fire, breaking the law of chastity, and driving while drunk. These choices can lead to life changing consequences for us and possibly others. When other people's choices lead to our lives becoming harder, we become victims whose futures are chosen for us. God does not want us to suffer these pains but sometimes allows them to happen for His own purposes.

The Pharaoh in this account was able to tell that the problems he had were due to his own actions. We know this because he doesn't tell Abram that it is all his fault. Instead, he takes responsibility for it and also figured out that the problems were a warning to prevent him from making further mistakes. I'll bet that in the future he was less likely to collect women than he had been so that he could avoid upsetting God again.

2. Hold others accountable for their actions.

Even though **we** know that Abram was commanded to lie about his relationship with Sarai **the Pharaoh in Genesis 12 probably did not have that knowledge when he was dealing with them**. After all it isn't always clear in the scriptures what details of the prophet's conversations with God are shared with others or kept to himself. If Sarai was the only person with whom Abram had shared God's commandment, then Pharaoh would have had to conclude that it was completely their idea and thus may have felt that the two of them had come into Egypt deliberately intending to deceive him. No one likes to be lied to. When confronting Abram, it is clear that this Pharaoh felt horror at the thought that he could have committed other sins because of the actions of these two. He confronts Abram about it holding him responsible for his part in the potential disaster. Good for him.

3) Beware of the hobbies that you take up.

Scholars and archeologists have determined that in some parts of the world it was a normal thing for kings and other wealthy people to have many wives and concubines. Just look at King Solomon. While this may have been culturally acceptable in their day, and may still be practiced in some parts of the world, this story shows that you cannot use cultural norms to justify breaking the commandments of God. Pharaoh could have played that card but he didn't showing integrity and accountability instead. If a king is willing to do that shouldn't all of us be as well?

27

Hagar - Mother of the Other Nations

When not in Egypt Abram/Abraham had daily contact with its culture through some of his servants including his wife's handmaiden Hagar[27]. When she entered the household is not clear, although she may have been one of the maidservants given to Abram by the Pharaoh in Genesis 12, nor is the extent of her relationship with either Abram/ Abraham or Sarai/Sarah. What is known is that after many years of marriage Abram and Sarai were still childless. To solve this problem Sarai came up with the idea of giving her handmaiden to Abram so that he could father a child through her.

"And Sarai said unto Abram, Behold now, the Lord hath restrained me from bearing: I pray thee, go in unto my maid; it may be that I may obtain children by her. And Abram hearkened to the voice of Sarai. And Sarai Abram's wife took Hagar her maid the Egyptian, after Abram had dwelt ten years in the land of Canaan, and gave her to her husband Abram to be his wife."[28]

Now we find ourselves at a loss here for several reasons because the actions of these people are so foreign to us here in the west. Hagar was a servant, and apparently treated as property, but still she was a person with rights wasn't she? Didn't she have a say in all of this? Apparently not because, like Bilhah and Zilpah in Genesis 30, we have nothing recorded regarding her being asked if she was willing to participate in this plan. Instead, she is simply given to Abram for the sole purpose of acting as a vessel for children which Sarai would then adopt as her own. While the prospect of motherhood may have been exciting, having no claim on her child probably wasn't. Most women want to raise their own children after all and not be forced to give them away.

Another issue would be how she felt about Abram. Hagar was probably quite young, possibly even a teenager (after all she was obviously in peak fertility time here or else they would not have considered her for this purpose), and apparently not married. Given their age difference and the fact that he was already married, she may never have considered Abram as a potential spouse and may in fact have been in love with someone else - after all she wasn't the only Egyptian servant that Abram and Sarai had. On the other hand, maybe she was happy with the arrangement because she was in love with Abram and didn't think that she would ever have a chance with him because of his devotion to his existing wife.

Another person in this scenario that raises questions is Sarai. Now I know that in the last chapter I said that scholars will point out that having multiple wives was not uncommon in that area or in antiquity in general, and it is still a custom practiced in some countries today, but I refuse to believe that

all women were okay with this custom. Even in modern times people don't always agree with all the customs and practices that are "normal" where they live but may often accept them with resignation as the way things are. In Abram and Sarai's case, the text doesn't say that he already had another wife so we can assume that at the time he wasn't practicing polygamy. If they went through with this then she would have to partially share him with someone else. How did she feel about that? They had been married for a very long time and may have become extremely close. She may have never had to share him with anyone before so this would be new territory for both of them.

Another thing I wonder about is how Sarai felt regarding the way that they would need to go about getting that child. How did she feel knowing that in order for her to be able to adopt a child her husband would have to "know" someone else? Did she resent knowing that Hagar would feel the joy of carrying a child whereas she had not yet been able to do that? Many modern women have a problem with the concept of using surrogates or other fertility treatments to overcome their fertility issues let alone having their husband or partner actually sleep with someone else. You also can't help but wonder if her barrenness made her feel like a failure and that this action was partly due to desperation.

While the text doesn't give us all of the answers to the above questions, modern revelation shows that this plan wasn't completely Sarai's idea. "God commanded Abraham, and Sarah gave Hagar to Abraham to wife. And why did she do it? Because this was the law; **and from Hagar sprang many people**. This, therefore, was fulfilling, among other things, the promises. Was Abraham, therefore, under condemnation? Verily I say unto you, Nay; for I, the Lord, commanded it." [29] OK so Sarai was being obedient to a commandment of the Lord. That makes a bit more sense. Even so, this commandment, like the one Abraham later received to sacrifice their son Isaac, may have been a difficult one for her to obey. Nevertheless, she did it and good for her for obeying under possibly difficult circumstances.

Now let's go back and look at the ultimate planner in this situation - God. What reasons did he have for this commandment? One of the promises given to Abraham was that through his descendants "all the families of the earth [would] be blessed".[30] Now if only one line was eligible for these blessings would this promise be fulfilled? Of course not. Hagar would help fulfil this promise by becoming the mother of one of Abraham's eight sons allowing for many other nations besides Israel to claim some of the blessings of the Abrahamic covenant. That the word wife is used to describe their union is also indicative of the honour of all of the people involved and their obedience to other commandments of God. Heavenly Father never condones his servants in breaking the law of chastity. Out of His desire for us to be happy He has said that "the sacred powers of procreation are to be employed only between man and woman, lawfully wedded as husband and wife."[31]

Although it doesn't mention a marriage ceremony one may have occurred and as Abram's wife they would not be breaking this law and Hagar would have some rights in the situation even though she would not be on the same level as Sarai/Sarah.

UNLIKELY RIGHTEOUSNESS: UNSUNG HEROES OF GENESIS

Now enough with the speculation for a minute. Let's get back to the story. So, Abraham and Hagar "knew" one another in the scriptural sense and the plan worked - she conceived. Unfortunately, her success in conceiving lead to a new problem for this love triangle.

"And [Abram] went in unto Hagar, and she conceived: and when she saw that she had conceived, her mistress [Sarai] was despised in her eyes."[32]

To despise someone is to "look down on with contempt or aversion: disdain, detest; to regard as negligible, worthless, or distasteful."[33] Whatever her feelings towards Sarai had been before all of this happened they were not friendly now. Basically, either she hated Sarai, considered herself more important because she had succeeded where her mistress had failed, or didn't feel the need to serve her the way she had before. All we know for sure is that Hagar and Sarai's relationship had significantly changed and Sarai did not like it.

"And Sarai said unto Abram, My wrong be upon thee: I have given my maid into thy bosom; and when she saw that she had conceived, I was despised in her eyes: the Lord judge between me and thee. But Abram said unto Sarai, Behold, thy maid is in thy hand; do to her as it pleaseth thee. And when Sarai dealt hardly with her, she fled from her face."[34]

One can only guess what else may have been said as part of this conversation. My guess would be that the recorder of Genesis did abbreviate it immensely because, having seen numerous married couples that have strong bonds between themselves and God, it is very rare that their conversations are this short - even if they are currently mad and not talking to each other. The other reason I suspect that there was more going on than is recorded is because of Abraham's response. Chances are good that, although imperfect, Sarai was a Christ-like noblewoman who was used to being liked and respected. She seems confused by the fact that her obedience to God's commandment has led to this situation with her handmaid. In her mind it doesn't appear that she feels she had done Hagar any disservice that would justify mistreatment. She may also have been struggling with the age difference and cultural differences between herself and Hagar leaving her baffled at her maid's attitude and unable to get her to come around.

Her complaint to her husband seems to be more along the lines of "I've tried everything I can think of and she is still [insert unnamed inappropriate behaviour here]! You are the head of the household - deal with this!" His response in turn appears to be "Wife, you are my second in command and she has not taken away your authority. She is under your stewardship and you should know by now how to deal with her. Try something else if you are still having problems."

Whether Hagar was present during this conversation isn't indicated nor is Sarai's chosen punishment. It is highly doubtful that she beat Hagar however since, after going through all of the trouble to get her pregnant so that they could adopt her child, neither she nor Abram would want to risk the girl's pregnancy. Starving her is also unlikely for the same reason. Whatever it was though must have been out of the ordinary because the girl feels the need to flee, while pregnant, into the wilderness. Going into the wilderness by herself under normal circumstances would have been dangerous so she must have felt pretty desperate to want to do it while pregnant. That leads us to wonder what was going on in her head? Did she love Abram and thought that she was going to become equal to or replace Sarai only to have that dream shattered? Was she angry because they had used her in a way that she hadn't wanted to be a part of and had been fighting back the only way she thought that she could? Did she feel betrayed because her previously loved mistress had laid down the law and she didn't feel like she deserved it? Did she feel alone and that no one understood her position? Was she just moody because her hormones were acting up and she didn't know how to handle it?[35] I don't know. What we do know is that God was watching this drama unfold and made sure that she was not harmed while in the vulnerable position she had put herself in.

"And the angel of the Lord found her by a fountain of water in the wilderness, by the fountain in the way to Shur."[36]

What a great honour to Hagar that she received an angelic visitation. While many people believe that they have a guardian angel most of us do not get the opportunity to see or talk to them. An angelic visit like this is more the exception than the norm. That's the reason it was recorded - the author wants us to know about Hagar's conversation with a messenger of God. Aside from the normal reason for an angelic visitation, that is to provide information, the angel may have been sent to Hagar for a more practical purpose. Depending on Hagar's state of mind when she ran away - having Abram, Sarai, or another member of the household come after her to try to get her to go back probably would not have worked out so well. People under emotional duress often don't think very clearly and can react unpredictably. It's entirely possible that she may have done something even more foolish in her efforts to get away thus putting herself in more danger or actually causing herself harm. Heavenly Father knew this and so He sent an outsider to talk to her.

"And he (the angel) said, Hagar, Sarai's maid, whence camest thou? and whither wilt thou go? And she said, I flee from the face of my mistress Sarai. And the angel of the Lord said unto her, Return to thy mistress, and submit thyself under her hands."[37]

We have no way of knowing what Hagar's belief structure had been up to this point. After all, just because she lived in the household of a prophet of God did not mean that she had accepted his teachings about God or was following them. She may very well have been following the religion of the Egyptians and had a "let's agree to disagree" opinion regarding the existence of Abraham's God when interacting with her masters. If that was the case then she definitely couldn't argue with God's existence after this conversation. As with many angelic visits this one seems to have been sudden enough so that she was caught by surprise and powerful enough that the angel has her full attention.

The angel shows Heavenly Father's intimate knowledge of her by the things he asks and the things he tells her. The question the angel asks her may have been an attempt to get her thinking rationally. If she had come from Egypt, then she was a long way from home and, as a servant, probably didn't have the best navigation skills in the world. From her response, it appears that her flight was so swift that she hadn't taken her final destination or the potential dangers she would face in the wilderness into account. Chances are good that after their initial exchange her thoughts were along the lines of "Hmm. He's right. Where am I going? I better consider that."

And then a bombshell - go back and submit to your mistress. Most likely being told that she needed to go back and resume her role as servant was not what Hagar had been expecting or what she wanted to hear. She may have felt that the way she had treated Sarai was completely justified and instead expected the Lord to agree with her. It is a gentle rebuke because Heavenly Father isn't justifying Hagar's behaviour towards Sarai and He is somewhat acknowledging that Sarai was right to reprimand her. He loved them both and wanted them both to be happy and as part of His plan Hagar needed to continue living in Abram's household. That was God's message to her and the angel obediently delivered it. Now it was up to Hagar to decide what she was going to do. She had a lot to think about.

One of the things that I find especially touching is that while her mind was probably still churning with the above thoughts and questions, the Angel goes one step further with His message from God and gives her two gifts:

- knowledge about her own future, and
- knowledge about her child and his future.

"And the angel of the Lord said unto her, I will multiply thy seed exceedingly, that it shall not be numbered for multitude. And the angel of the Lord said unto her, Behold, thou art with child, and shalt bear a son, and shalt call his name Ishmael; **because the Lord hath heard thy affliction**. And he will be a wild man; his hand will be against every man, and every man's hand against him; and he shall dwell in the presence of all his brethren."[38]

Now for those of you who are paying attention and have come to know a bit about the Abrahamic covenant (or just remember what I said earlier about it) this is where Hagar is given one of the same promises as Abraham regarding her descendants. Abraham wasn't the only one who could claim them. She was promised that her line would live on and that she would have innumerable descendants. She is also told that she is having a son - something that she would have had no way of knowing until the delivery - and what to name him. The most personal thing that she was told, something that those who have had their prayers answered know well, is that God had heard her. If having an angel visit her hadn't touched her heart just by itself hearing this and knowing it was true did. God had heard her - Hagar. A nobody from an earthly perspective and yet a precious daughter, known by name and loved by her Heavenly Father. Her response shows her gratitude for these gifts and a change in her attitude.

"And she called the name of the Lord that spake unto her, Thou God seest me: for she said, Have I also here looked after him that seeth me?"[39]

If she hadn't been a follower of Abram's God before she definitely was one now. After thanking the Lord for His help, she follows the angel's advice and goes back to her master and mistress, completes her pregnancy, and has the son promised her. Yay!

"And Hagar bare Abram a son: and Abram called his son's name, which Hagar bare, Ishmael. And Abram was fourscore and six [86] years old, when Hagar bare Ishmael to Abram."[40]

One of the things I find fascinating in the scriptures is when the text gives us multiple stories about a person so we can see how they grow and change over time. Unfortunately, the next time we hear about Hagar things are still not ideal for her. This is because one of the problems that we find in life is that the larger the household the greater the chance that people do not get along. We shouldn't fault the participants too much because, like us, they are imperfect and have their own emotional struggles. Several years after having Ishmael, Sarah's barrenness comes to an end and she is able to conceive and have a son of her own - Isaac. Happy Day for both Abraham and Sarah. Not such a great day for Hagar and Ishmael.

"Wherefore [Sarah] said unto Abraham, Cast out this bondwoman [Hagar] and her son [Ishmael]: for the son of this bondwoman shall not be heir with my son, even with Isaac."[41]

This sounds harsh but we must understand something for it to make sense. In their culture the oldest son of the principal wife inherited his father's estate. Therefore, although Ishmael was significantly older he had lost his place as heir when Isaac was born since he was the son of the second wife. Too bad for him in this instance. Abraham's reaction to Sarah's request this time isn't quite so calm. Unlike last time Sarah came to him with a complaint about Hagar we learn that "the thing **was very grievous** in Abraham's sight because of his son."[42] While we don't know how he felt about Hagar obviously he loved Ishmael and didn't want to see him go. Once again Heavenly Father steps in and provides a bit of comfort and insight.

"And God said unto Abraham, Let it not be grievous in thy sight because of the lad, and because of thy bondwoman; in all that Sarah hath said unto thee, hearken unto her voice; for in Isaac shall thy seed be called. **And also of the son of the bondwoman will I make a nation, because he is thy seed.**" [43]

Even with the insight that it was all part of God's plan and everything would be okay - this STILL had to be a difficult thing for Abraham to do. These are the days before mass communication and travel. By casting them out Abraham knew that he would probably never see his son again in this life. That had to hurt. Yet, showing his ever willingness to obey, he went through with it and sent them on their way.

"And Abraham rose up early in the morning, and took bread, and a bottle of water, and gave it unto Hagar, putting it on her shoulder, and the child, and sent her away: and she departed, and wandered in the wilderness of Beer-sheba."[44]

Hagar is back in the wilderness and this time it isn't by choice. At least this time she isn't alone - she has her teenage son with her. Again, we have to consider what she may have been thinking. She was older and wiser, now had more than herself to think about, and had to wonder all of the whys about the situation. She must have been confused over the events that had just transpired - again we don't know if Abraham shared with her the fact that this was in accordance with Heavenly Father's Plan or not. She was probably grateful that they had some provisions for their journey but had to know after living in the desert for many years that one bottle of water wasn't going to last very long. She would most likely have been missing the comfort of being with her countrymen and women and possibly the standard of living she had enjoyed as a member of Abraham's household. All that we know is that she wandered around until they eventually ran out of water.

"And the water was spent in the bottle, and she cast the child under one of the shrubs."[45]

Unlike how she felt about leaving Abraham's household during her previous departure into the wilderness, the next few verses give us insight into her state of mind when the water ran out.

"And she went, and sat her down over against him a good way off, as it were a bowshot: for she said, Let me not see the death of the child. And she sat over against him, and lift up her voice, and wept."[46]

Hagar was scared. She was out of water, obviously did not know where to find more, and her son was going to suffer as a result. As a mother she probably had a great desire to provide and protect her child from anything that would cause him harm however due to circumstances beyond her control she was currently unable to do that. This was a desperate situation and I can't blame her for turning her back when she was sure that they were both going to die. I wouldn't want to witness the death of my child either. Fortunately for her God was once again watching over her and would make sure that the two of them would be all right.

"And God heard the voice of the lad; and the angel of God called to Hagar out of heaven, and said unto her, What aileth thee, Hagar? **fear not**; for God hath heard the voice of the lad where he is. Arise, lift up the lad, and hold him in thine hand; for I will make him a great nation."[47]

Once again Heavenly Father reached out and comforted His beloved daughter and her son during their time of need. He also reminded her of who He is and what promises He had made to her. Her earlier conversation with the angel showed that she had believed Him and His promises at the time but in her current distressed state she appears to have forgotten. We shouldn't blame her though because faith in God is a never-ending process and Hagar's may have become slightly shaky at this time making it difficult for her to see how His promises would work out. This angelic message is a gentle reminder that God was in control and that all would be well - and it was.

"And God opened her eyes, and she saw a well of water; and she went, and filled the bottle with water, and gave the lad drink. And God was with the lad; and he grew, and dwelt in the wilderness, and became an archer. And he dwelt in the wilderness of Paran: and his mother took him a wife out of the land of Egypt."[48]

This is where Hagar's story ends. We do not know how long she lived, where she may have resided until her death, or if she ever married again and had more children. Hagar's story is inspirational because it shows that God is always watching us and willing to help us. He corrects us when necessary and provides us with the help that we need. Now - what lessons can we learn from her?

1. God is no respecter of persons.

Heavenly Father is not like us - he does not play favorites. If He did then He would only have cared about Abraham and Sarah and would have not included Hagar, an Egyptian, in His plan to bless all of the families of the Earth. That she, and other people, were included in this plan shows that in the eyes of God there is no differences between the races. All people are welcome to come unto Him as long as they are willing to accept His teachings and obey His commandments.

2. Our reasons do not equal excuses.

As mentioned above Hagar was gently rebuked by the first angel she met while pregnant for the way she had been acting prior to her run into the wilderness. The angel doesn't yell at her nor does he condone her behaviour but instead tells her to go back and submit to her mistress. God is all knowing and understands the reasons behind our actions usually better than we do. Even though Hagar may have felt justified, been young and immature, and/or some of her behaviour may have been due to her pregnancy it did not make her treatment of Sarai/ Sarah correct. Without actually saying it the angel tells her the same thing that Jesus Christ centuries later told the woman taken in adultery "Neither do I condemn thee: go, and sin no more."[49]

3. Our future may be glorious and we will not know it until we are humble enough to have it revealed to us by God.

Hagar's background and alternative futures will always be a mystery to us. As with any historical person the what ifs are infinite because any change in behaviour may very well have caused huge changes in the outcome. If she hadn't been chosen for this specific purpose, she may have died in obscurity with not even her name known to us. By being a participant in the story to bring about the "Abrahamic Covenant" Hagar's name is not only known but she became the matriarch of several nations and was able to claim some of the promised blessings for herself and her descendants. It was only due to her humility in the dessert when she was first approached by an angel of God that she found these things out. Given that the human spirit is eternal one can't help but wonder what else she has done since her time on Earth came to an end.

Abimelech - A King
for All Ages

Although I am trying not to be biased as I write about these unheralded heroic people, I have to admit that Abimelech is one of my favorite people found in the Bible. We are fortunate because the text provides us with more information about the things he did and said over several years allowing us to draw more conclusions about his character than other people covered in this book. He is also unique in that he was able to meet with not only Abraham but Isaac as well allowing him to befriend and potentially influence two of the founding patriarchs of the Israelite nation. Intrigued yet? Well let's find out about this great man.

Abimelech story starts off in the same place that several other kings do - Abraham was living a nomadic life and his travels lead him to Abimelech's country. The text says that this land was in "the south country... between Kadesh and Shur... in Gerar"[50] which made him a king of the Philistines. Now remember that problem that Abraham had in Genesis 12 with having a beautiful wife that he was afraid other men might kill him for? Well, we have to assume it was still a concern for him because he tells Abimilech the same story he told the Genesis 12 Pharaoh.

"And Abraham said of Sarah his wife, She is my sister: and Abimelech king of Gerar sent, and took Sarah."[51]

Now for those of you who are wondering where I'm going with this I do have a point. Thus far we have the same scenario - wife is taken by king of the country. Nothing new there but the text tells us more - this time, unlike the Pharaoh in Genesis 12, we know that Heavenly Father warned the king about the truth of the situation before he sinned any more. This shows us a lot about Abimelech. What do I mean? Well read on.

"But God came to Abimelech in a dream by night, and said to him, Behold, thou art but a dead man, for the woman which thou hast taken; for she is a man's wife. But Abimelech had not come near her: and he said, Lord, wilt thou slay also a righteous nation? Said he not unto me, She is my sister? and she, even she herself said, He is my brother: **in the integrity of my heart and innocency of my hands have I done this**. And God said unto him in a dream, **Yea, I know that thou didst this in the integrity of thy heart**; for I also withheld thee from sinning against me: therefore suffered I thee not to touch her. Now therefore restore the man his wife; for he is a prophet, and he shall pray for thee, and thou shalt live: and if thou restore her not, know thou that thou shalt surely die, thou, and all that are thine."[52]

Now there are a few things I'd like to point out from this little "dream conversation":

- Abimelech **knew** God.

Abimelech is not surprised, tongue-tied, or confused by this exchange nor does he wake up shaking so, just like with Cain, we have to assume that he and Heavenly Father had talked before. Also, unlike with Hagar, no angel is sent to him to deliver the message - God converses with Abimelech **himself** through a dream. This shows that Abimelech was special and deeply cared for by God and that Abimelech loved Him right back as he does not show any rebelliousness when rebuked. That this relationship occurred is confusing to us because this man is a Philistine. Later in the Bible the Philistines are a Pagan nation and enemies of the Israelites. What is he doing having an intimate relationship with God? How and when it started isn't important. What is important is that they did know and love each other.

- Abimelech respected the law of chastity.

While we do not know why he took Sarah into his household, other than that he thought she was Abraham's sister, the text tells us that he had "not come near her". Unlike Julius Caesar and other rulers who seemed to feel that they were not men unless they slept with every woman that they came in contact with Abimelech and Sarah had not had sex nor does it appear that he had made any inappropriate behaviours towards her. This allowed him to have confidence when he spoke with the Lord and explained himself. It is also evident that the Lord knew that Abimelech respected this law since He warns him before he **has a chance to break it**.

- Abimelech knew that he had not sinned deliberately.

The phrase "in the integrity of my heart and innocency of my hands" used by Abimelech when he is explaining himself would have been a dangerous excuse to use when speaking to a god that knows everything **if it were not true**. Nevertheless, Abimelech says it with confidence showing that it was a fact. The Lord also confirms that his motivations had been to do good even though his actions may not have been perfectly right. That the Lord is warning him shows us that Abimelech often strived to do the right thing in the eyes of the Lord and the Lord wanted him to continue doing so.

- Abimelech knew God's character.

Abimelech knew that God is both just and merciful. The threat on his life was not a guaranteed thing but a warning of what would happen if he didn't repent.

We know this because during the conversation he asks the Lord if he would "slay a righteous nation?" Of course not. God only destroys those nations and people that have completely turned their backs on Him, are spiritually destroying themselves, and have the potential to influence other people to spiritual destruction. God rewards Abimelech's trust in Him by telling him how he could correct the situation and then leaves the decision up to him.

Now other than the fact that God loved him enough to warn him Abimelech shows what a great leader he was from here on out. Some people may have woken up and not acted on their dream. Abimelech was not one of these people. Instead he "rose early in the morning, and called all his servants, and told all these things in their ears: and the men were sore afraid." [53] He acted immediately starting off by letting his servants, those who answered to him, know the reasons for the odd occurrences they had been experiencing (later on in Genesis 20:17-18 we learn that his entire household was barren). That the servants were "sore afraid" shows that they realised the dream was from God as well. Then Abimelech calls the source of his problems to him and asks for an explanation.

"Then Abimelech called Abraham, and said unto him, What hast thou done unto us? and **what have I offended thee, that thou hast brought on me and on my kingdom a great sin**? thou hast done deeds unto me that ought not to be done. And Abimelech said unto Abraham, What sawest thou, that thou hast done this thing?"[54]

Although he had not sinned intentionally Abimelech shows honour by admitting that he had done wrong in taking a married woman away from her husband. I also can't help but wonder if there wasn't hurt in his voice when he said these things to Abraham. Here's why. Abraham and Sarah must have been there **at least** six months to a year or more for Abimelech and his household to have realised that they were suffering the plague of bareness. After all the barrenness may not have just affected the humans but the animals as well and animals are bred during specific seasons. During that time Abraham would have had the chance to get to know him. When reading between the lines I hear Abimelech saying "I trusted you and have tried to be a friend unto you. How could you betray me like this? Why weren't **you** the one to tell me the truth? Why did God have to be the one to do it?" And then he gets the exact same answer that kings have gotten so far to these questions for several chapters in Genesis.

"And Abraham said, Because I thought, Surely the fear of God is not in this place; and they will slay me for my wife's sake. And yet indeed she is my sister; she is the daughter of my father, but not the daughter of my mother; and she became my wife. And it came to pass, when God caused me to wander from my father's house, that I said unto her, This is thy kindness which thou shalt shew unto me; at every place whither we shall come, say of me, He is my brother."[55]

I will not judge Abraham for telling half-truths. Besides that we have already established he was obeying a commandment from the Lord, we cannot possibly have all of the records of his travels. For all I know he had been to places where this half-truth **had** saved his and Sarah's lives because the people did not follow the commandments of God nor respect the authority of God so Abraham's fear of being killed because of her may have been very real to him. I do feel for Abimelech though because for the rest of his history as recorded in the Bible his actions show that he did not fall into this category and I agree with him - Abraham should have recognised that the fear of the Lord was in that place and told him the truth.

"And Abimelech took sheep, and oxen, and menservants, and womenservants, and gave them unto Abraham, and restored him Sarah his wife. And Abimelech said, Behold, my land is before thee: dwell where it pleaseth thee."[56]

Abimelech must have believed the Lord's promises because he doesn't ask Abraham to leave but instead invites him to be a permanent guest. Another reason that I like how he handles the situation is that not only does he hold himself and Abraham accountable but also Sarah showing that he recognised that she had some responsibility in all of this as well.

"And unto Sarah he said, Behold, I have given thy brother a thousand pieces of silver: behold, he is to thee a covering of the eyes, unto all that are with thee, and with all other: **thus she was reproved**."[57] To reprove is to "to administer a rebuke to; to express disapproval of **synonyms,** reprimand, admonish, reproach, chide."[58] As a member of Abimelech's household Sarah would most likely have had greater opportunities than Abraham to learn his character, either from her interactions with him directly or by talking to his family members, and see that he did in fact fear the Lord. Unless they had both been commanded to never reveal their true relationship under any circumstances then she did not have to remain silent but could have told Abimelech the truth. She was just as culpable as Abraham and deserved to be reprimanded as well.

Now that Abimelech had passed the test having done what the Lord had told him to do it was Abraham's turn to fulfill his role as prophet. "So Abraham prayed unto God: and God healed Abimelech, and his wife, and his maidservants; and they bare children. For the Lord had fast closed up all the wombs of the house of Abimelech, because of Sarah Abraham's wife."[59] Yay! Everything is back to normal.

Fast forward an undisclosed amount of time and we have another opportunity to view and admire Abimelech.

"And it came to pass at that time, that Abimelech and Phichol the chief captain of his host spake unto Abraham, saying, **God is with thee in all that thou doest**: Now therefore swear unto me here by God that thou wilt not deal falsely with me, nor with my son, nor with my son's son: but according to the kindness that I have done unto thee, thou shalt do unto me, and to the land wherein thou hast sojourned."[60]

His relationship with God allowed Abimelech to recognise other men and women of God. While we do not know what specific behaviour had prompted this statement we can assume that Abraham had showed through his actions where his loyalties lay. Abimelech wanted his family and his people to be successful so during an official visit he and his chief captain proposed an alliance. By this time it appears that Abraham has learned for himself that Abimelech is also a man of God because he has no problems with the proposal however he does have a complaint against Abimelech's servants.

"And Abraham said, I will swear. And Abraham reproved Abimelech because of a well of water, which Abimelech's servants had violently taken away."[61]

This is a legitimate complaint. We are in the desert/semi-desert remember and access to water is very important. Even today there can be conflicts and even wars between countries due to water shortages or access to pure water. This confrontation didn't escalate however because the two parties worked it out quickly and to the satisfaction of them both.

"And Abimelech said, I wot not who hath done this thing: neither didst thou tell me, neither yet heard I of it, but to day. And Abraham took sheep and oxen, and gave them unto Abimelech; and both of them made a covenant. And Abraham set seven ewe lambs of the flock by themselves. And Abimelech said unto Abraham, What mean these seven ewe lambs which thou hast set by themselves? And he said, For these seven ewe lambs shalt thou take of my hand, that they may be a witness unto me, that I have digged this well. Wherefore he called that place Beer-sheba; because there they sware both of them. Thus they made a covenant at Beer-sheba: then Abimelech rose up, and Phichol the chief captain of his host, and they returned into the land of the Philistines."[62]

I like this conversation in the scriptures for two reasons:

Reason 1 - Abimelech is a good leader even though he does not know everything.

While I agree that Abraham had a legitimate complaint regarding his well, he should have taken it up with Abimelech before this conversation. This is the second time that Abimelech defends himself in such a way that it implies he would have responded differently with more information. He didn't know about his servants actions so how could he reprimand them? His willingness to make a covenant with Abraham indicates that that is the direction he would have gone if he had all of the info. He is an imperfect man that is going with the information that he has available at the time.

The other thing to note is that Abimelech initiated this as an official meeting not a back door gathering where things can be denied later on. True he may have taken Phichol with him for protection as he travelled to meet with Abraham but based on what we've seen so far I think that there was another reason he did it. By taking Phichol with him he would have a witness to not only what Abraham agreed to **but what he did as well**. Think about it, the first people he is recorded to have told his dream from God to were not just his wife, courtiers, or another person of high rank but **all of his servants**. While we don't know if he was beloved by his people the fact that he cared about making sure that they had all of the information makes me think that he **was** liked and respected by them. The presence of this witness would keep him accountable because if he went back on his word he would lose the respect of his people and possibly his power as their king as well.

Reason 2 - Everybody wins in the scenario.

This conversation shows a win-win situation. Abimelech knew that by keeping Abraham with him he would be able to continue learning from him and receive more blessings from God. Abraham on the other hand wanted the well he dug returned to him. By making a covenant with each other Abimelech insured the future for himself and his descendants while Abraham had the king's official acknowledgement of what belonged to him which he could use in future conflicts if he had to. It is apparent that they both liked, respected and trusted each other so they also won because the friendship that they had been building up to this point could continue as Abraham would remain nearby.

Abimelech's reign lasted a long time because as mentioned before he was able to interact with two of the patriarchs. Now I'd like to make a note that I have no definitive proof that the man that met Isaac is in fact the same man that met Abraham however I do believe that he was for several reasons which I will cover later in the text. If it was in fact the same man then two things are apparent:

1. Abraham obviously never mentioned to Isaac that Abimelech and his people feared God; and
2. Abimelech has no luck with this family being honest with him when they first enter his country.

"And Isaac dwelt in Gerar: And the men of the place asked him of his wife; and he said, She is my sister: for he feared to say, She is my wife; lest, said he, the men of the place should kill me for Rebekah; because she was fair to look upon. And it came to pass, **when he had been there a long time**, that Abimelech king of the Philistines looked out at a window, and saw, and, behold, Isaac was sporting with Rebekah his wife."[63]

Like father like son - "you're my sister whenever we enter a new place. Got it?". Now to be fair Isaac may have received the same commandment from God to say his wife was his sister in order to protect himself. It's entirely possible. The fact that this scenario is repeating itself is humorous in a sad way because poor Abimelech. Now it doesn't say that he took her into his household this time but he obviously believed Isaac and Rebekah so this must have come as a shock to him to catch them in their lie like that. It doesn't say how they explained their children though so maybe he had suspected something. The other thing that is humorous is how he finds out the truth. The Bible is discreet in that all it says is that they were "sporting" with each other so we have no idea exactly what that means (they were in public though so it couldn't have been too extreme) but whatever was happening was **obviously** not the way brothers and sisters behave towards each other, no matter how close the family is.

OK time for another confrontation.

"And Abimelech called Isaac, and said, Behold, of a surety she is thy wife: and how saidst thou, She is my sister? And Isaac said unto him, Because I said, Lest I die for her. And Abimelech said, What is this thou hast done unto us? one of the people might lightly have lien with thy wife, and thou shouldest have brought guiltiness upon us."[64]

UNLIKELY RIGHTEOUSNESS: UNSUNG HEROES OF GENESIS

Is anyone else experiencing déja vu? This is almost the exact same conversation Abimelech had with Isaac's father. Same concern from Abimelech (law of chastity could have been broken) and same reason from the man in question (you could have killed me because she is so beautiful). Sigh. You have to give Isaac and Rebekah credit for tenacity though because it says that they had been there a long time. How long we don't know but as they appeared to enjoy being a married couple it must have been harder for them to keep the ruse going as time went by. No wonder they cracked.

"And Abimelech charged all his people, saying, He that toucheth this man or his wife shall surely be put to death."[65]

Once again Abimelech protects his guests even though they lied to him. Over time Isaac is blessed by the Lord and becomes very wealthy.[66] So wealthy in fact that Abimelech sends him away.

"And Abimelech said unto Isaac, Go from us; for thou art much mightier than we."[67]

As requested, Isaac left and continued to build his wealth. Eventually, his works and actions come to the attention of Abimelech and another official meeting is called, this time with two witnesses.

"Then Abimelech went to him from Gerar, and Ahuzzath one of his friends, and Phichol the chief captain of his army. And Isaac said unto them, Wherefore come ye to me, seeing ye hate me, and have sent me away from you? And they said, **We saw certainly that the Lord was with thee**: and we said, Let there be now an oath betwixt us, even betwixt us and thee, and let us make a covenant with thee; That thou wilt do us no hurt, as we have not touched thee, and as we have done unto thee nothing but good, and have sent thee away in peace: thou art now the blessed of the Lord."[68]

Now here is why I am convinced that this is the same man. While it is possible that both Abimelech and Phichol could have named their sons after themselves, and that said sons could have been the ones in this account, the consistency of the words and actions of this king leads me to believe he was the same one that met with Abraham. If that is true he may have sent Isaac away for a couple of reasons:

1. it is possible that he had felt incredibly betrayed by Isaac and Rebekah's lie and didn't think he could trust them again;
2. Maybe the wealth of Isaac really did make them nervous. After all money can lead to weapons and war so, if he didn't know where Isaac's loyalties lay, he may have feared him joining with his enemies; and/or
3. It could have been a test for Isaac to prove that like his father Abraham he was a man committed to and favored by God and thereby one to stay on the good side of.

Whatever the reason(s) we can see that this visit was due to their recognising that he was favored by the Lord and wanting him to acknowledge that they had treated him fairly. We don't know if the king was aware of the conflicts over water between

Isaac's servants and his people as it is not mentioned but his request is acceptable to Isaac and they made their own covenant.

"And he made them a feast, and they did eat and drink. And they rose up betimes in the morning, and sware one to another: and Isaac sent them away, and they departed from him in peace. And it came to pass the same day, that Isaac's servants came, and told him concerning the well which they had digged, and said unto him, We have found water. And he called it Shebah: therefore the name of the city is Beer-sheba unto this day."[69]

What a great man and an example to leaders today. What can we learn from Abimelech?

1. Leaders do not need to be perfect.

Abimelech made many mistakes in this story due to a lack of information and his own imperfections. This did not dissuade him from continuing to lead his people to the best of his ability. His relationship with the Lord gave him two advantages over other kings both then and now: a) he was able to know who to make alliances with so that his people would prosper, and b) he had access to the source of all knowledge and thus, as long as he was humble, could get any information that he needed to overcome the weaknesses that he already had. His honesty with his people and his guests and his willingness to hold himself accountable when necessary also helped him as a leader because others knew that they could trust him.

2. The decisions of others will affect you.

Was the plague of bareness given to Abimelech's household for taking Sarah away from Abraham fair? Well, the answer is both yes and no. From an earthly perspective punishing him for something that he did with the right intentions does not seem fair. From a spiritual and justice perspective though it was completely fair. You may have heard the phrase "ignorance of the law is no excuse". While we have to alter it slightly because Abimelech was not ignorant of the laws of God - on the contrary he was dutifully trying to follow them - it does apply here. The decisions of Abraham, Sarah, Isaac, and Rebekah to lie about their true relationships left Abimelech ignorant of some of the circumstances in the stories we have for him and as a result he **did** break some of the Laws of God both through omission and commission. God could not overlook these and so did apply some punishment but stepped in to prevent Abimelech from causing himself too much harm.

3. Wealth does not always lead to corruption.

One of the most derogatory phrases used today is "the filthy rich". I find it derogatory because, like all stereotypic phrases, you can always find an exception. This phrase implies that all wealthy people are lazy, corrupt, greedy, cruel, think that the laws don't apply to them, etc. As a king Abimelech was probably very wealthy and powerful. Indeed, he would have had to be wealthy in order to still have servants and other possessions after giving some away to Abraham and yet his wealth does not appear in the slightest to have corrupted him. Instead, like many wealthy people who despite their imperfections use their power and influence for good, Abimelech cares about his duty to God, his responsibility to his people, and his friendships and alliances and uses his power to do good. If all kings and political leaders throughout history had been like him imagine how different the history of the earth could have been.

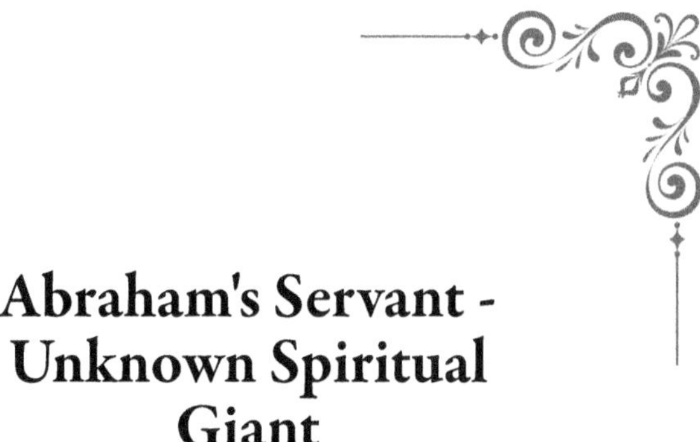

Abraham's Servant - Unknown Spiritual Giant

It has been said that "birds of a feather flock together" and I think that it is an appropriate phrase for this story. As mentioned already, Abraham was a very righteous man whose line had been chosen to change the fate of the human race by providing us with a Saviour who would enable us to overcome the effects of Adam's transgression and allow us to return to live with God. Because of this knowledge he was very aware of the importance of his son marrying the right person, who would share his beliefs and teach their children the same, and was willing to sacrifice in order to do it. Rather than allowing his son to marry one of the local girls, who could potentially lead him away from serving God, Abraham wanted to ensure that his son Isaac and his future daughter-in-law would have the same spiritual foundation.

Now the question facing Abraham is how do we go about doing it? Abraham had two problems. According to the text he "...was old, *and* well stricken in age.[70]" This phrase "was old" is actually an understatement. We know that he was 100 when his son Isaac was born[71] and that his wife Sarah, who was 10 years his junior, had died at 127[72] so since the story of her death and burial precedes this one Abraham must have been at least 137 when the question of his son's marriage arose. His other problem was that although there were probably many eligible women nearby **none** of them had the capacity and spiritual foundation necessary to be the right type of wife and mother that was needed so they would have to search elsewhere. Although it was not uncommon in the Book of Genesis for people to live well over 100 years, nor is he the only one that has to go away to find the right bride (Jacob does it later on as well), Abraham appears to be unable to do everything required to accomplish it so he does the next best thing - he sends someone he **trusts completely** to act on his behalf.

"And Abraham said unto his **eldest servant of his house, that ruled over all that he had**, Put, I pray thee, thy hand under my thigh: And I will make thee swear by the Lord, the God of heaven, and the God of the earth, that thou shalt not take a wife unto my son of the daughters of the Canaanites, among whom I dwell: But thou shalt go unto my country, and to my kindred, and take a wife unto my son Isaac."[73]

Wealthy people in order to build and maintain their wealth have learned how to become wise stewards. A wise steward, as Abraham must have been, wasn't just going to give this important assignment to just anybody. The person for the job would have proven that they were trustworthy, responsible, diligent, and most importantly had a great faith in God. Abraham's unnamed servant was such a man! In fact right off the bat he shows that he can think ahead because he recognises that there may be complications in getting the couple together so they could marry. He talks to Abraham about it and they come to an agreement that works for both of them.

"And the servant said unto him, Peradventure the woman will not be willing to follow me unto this land: must I needs bring thy son again unto the land from whence thou camest? And Abraham said unto him, Beware thou that thou bring not my son thither again. The Lord God of heaven, which took me from my father's house, and from the land of my kindred, and which spake unto me, and that sware unto me, saying, Unto thy seed will I give this land; he shall send his angel before thee, and thou shalt take a wife unto my son from thence. **And if the woman will not be willing to follow thee, then thou shalt be clear from this my oath: only bring not my son thither again.** And the servant put his hand under the thigh of Abraham his master, and sware to him concerning that matter." [74]

The servant in no way wanted to force the girl to come with him against her will nor did Abraham want his son to leave the land promised to him by the Lord. They are both confident however that God will assist the servant in his journey so shortly thereafter "the servant took ten camels of the camels of his master, and departed; for all the goods of his master were in his hand: and he arose, and went to Mesopotamia, unto the city of Nahor. And he made his camels to kneel down without the city by a well of water at the time of the evening, *even* the time that women go out to draw *water*."[75]

Now up to this point the servant has just shown that he is obedient, trustworthy, and can navigate effectively on a journey. Here is where he shows us the degree of faith that he has in God. The prayer he offers in the following verses is powerful and inspiring because it shows not only faith but experience as well. **This man knew how to pray to get results!**

"And he said, O Lord God of my master Abraham, I pray thee, send me good speed this day, and shew kindness unto my master Abraham. Behold, I stand *here* by the well of water; and the daughters of the men of the city come out to draw water: And let it come to pass, that the damsel to whom I shall say, Let down thy pitcher, I pray thee, that I may drink; and she shall say, Drink, and I will give thy camels drink also: *let the same be* she *that* thou hast appointed for thy servant Isaac; and thereby shall I know that thou hast shewed kindness unto my master." [76]

Often when I've talked about this story with others in the past they always say that Rebekah must have been an exceptional person to be willing to serve Abraham's servant, his entourage, and ten camels. I'm not going to argue with that - she was or else the Lord would not have chosen her to become Isaac's wife. The specificity of the request makes me think though that due to the hospitality rules of the time there may have been more than one girl that **could** have responded in this way. If that was the case then the servant was making sure that he knew which one was the right one without causing any of the girls he would come in contact with to feel uncomfortable. The servant is fortunate in that he doesn't have long to wait before he receives an answer to his prayer.

UNLIKELY RIGHTEOUSNESS: UNSUNG HEROES OF GENESIS

"And it came to pass, **before he had done speaking**, that, behold, Rebekah came out, who was born to Bethuel, son of Milcah, the wife of Nahor, Abraham's brother, with her pitcher upon her shoulder. And the damsel *was* very fair to look upon, a virgin, neither had any man known her: and she went down to the well, and filled her pitcher, and came up."[77]

Whether Rebekah was the first girl to approach the well or not is unclear. What the text does make clear is that she was eye catching. The Bible does not use the term "very fair" frequently nor does it use it loosely. This was a rare beauty. There must have been something else about her though because "the servant **ran to meet her**, and said, Let me, I pray thee, drink a little water of thy pitcher."[78]

He was a man who acted quickly and decisively. He didn't wait for her to approach him but ran to her. It wasn't just her beauty that he would have looked at either. A spiritual man like this would not have just looked on the external. He would have understood the lesson taught to Samuel that *"the Lord seeth* not as man seeth; for man looketh on the outward appearance, but the Lord looketh on the heart."[79] We all know that some "beautiful people" can be shallow or have other undesirable attributes that would have disqualified her from filling the important role he was there to ensure happened. To overcome this problem the man shows that he understood that we need to act first and then let God fulfill his part. He had done his part, now the test: if she responded the way that he had requested then she was the one for his master's son. She does not disappoint.

"And she said, Drink, my lord: and she hasted, and let down her pitcher upon her hand, and gave him drink. And when she had done giving him drink, she said, I will draw *water* for thy camels also, until they have done drinking. And she hasted, and emptied her pitcher into the trough, and ran again unto the well to draw *water*, and drew for all his camels."[80]

So far so good. She is beautiful, kind, and hard working. Now there is one more thing he needs to know before he can be sure she is the one God has sent him to bring back - is she from a lineage that will ensure she will teach her children about the One True God? Only one way to find out.

"And the man wondering at her held his peace, to wit whether the Lord had made his journey prosperous or not. And it came to pass, as the camels had done drinking, that the man took a golden earring of half a shekel weight, and two bracelets for her hands of ten *shekels* weight of gold; And said, **Whose daughter *art* thou? tell me, I pray thee: is there room *in* thy father's house for us to lodge in?**"[81]

Although it doesn't say it, he may have been holding his breath at this point because this is the moment of decision. If she answers incorrectly he now would have to wait until his camels are thirsty again or come up with another test to use to find the right girl. The suspense is killing us....

"And she said unto him, I *am* the daughter of Bethuel the son of Milcah, which she bare unto Nahor. She said moreover unto him, We have both straw and provender enough, and room to lodge in."[82]

Now if it had been me I may have shouted in delight and done a happy dance at this point. After all, he has just had another confirmation that Abraham worships the One True God and that God cares about all his children. Fortunately, the servant has more decorum than that.

"And the man bowed down his head, and worshipped the Lord. And he said, Blessed *be* the Lord God of my master Abraham, who hath not left destitute my master of his mercy and his truth: I *being* in the way, the Lord led me to the house of my master's brethren."[83]

Don't you just love him? This man is amazing. Not only did he willingly make this journey, pray specifically for a way to determine who he should look for, act quickly to ensure that he fulfilled his part in this test, and ask the right questions to get the final piece of information that he needed. Now to top it all off he is giving credit where the credit is due and praises the Lord. His praises have an unexpected effect though - she takes off!

"And the damsel ran..."[84] fortunately she didn't run far or out of fear "and told *them of* her mother's house these things." [85] Oh good now her family knows. Well the servant needed to speak to them anyway about a place to stay and about letting him take her back to his master so she can get married. Now it's time to meet the family. "And Rebekah had a brother, and his name *was* Laban: and Laban ran out unto the man, unto the well."[86] Her brother is here. How will he react?

"And it came to pass, when [Laban] saw the earring and bracelets upon his sister's hands, and when he heard the words of Rebekah his sister, saying, Thus spake the man unto me; that he came unto the man; and, behold, he stood by the camels at the well. And he said, Come in, **thou blessed of the Lord**; wherefore standest thou without? for I have prepared the house, and room for the camels."[87]

Now many of us after a long voyage with only water to drink up to this point would probably want a nap, a good meal, and/or to just relax and recuperate. This man probably did also want these things - he is human after all - however he knew his mission and he knew that it had not as yet been completed so he had other more important things on his mind.

"And the man came into the house: and he ungirded his camels, and gave straw and provender for the camels, and water to wash his feet, and the men's feet that *were* with him. And there was set *meat* before him to eat: but he said, **I will not eat, until I have told mine errand**."[88]

Being good hosts they let him say what he had to say. It is a long story.

"And [Laban] said, Speak on. And [the servant] said, I *am* Abraham's servant. And the Lord hath blessed my master greatly; and he is become great: and he hath given him flocks, and herds, and silver, and gold, and menservants, and maidservants, and camels, and asses. And Sarah my master's wife bare a son to my master when she was old: and unto him hath he given all that he hath. And my master made me swear, saying, Thou shalt not take a wife to my son of the daughters of the Canaanites, in whose land I dwell: But thou shalt go unto my father's house, and to my kindred, and take a wife unto my son. And I said unto my master, Peradventure the woman will not follow me. And he said unto me, The Lord, before whom I walk, will send his angel with thee, and prosper thy way; and thou shalt take a wife for my son of my kindred, and of my father's house: Then shalt thou be clear from *this* my oath, when thou comest to my kindred; and if they give not thee *one,* thou shalt be clear from my oath. And I came this day unto the well, and said, O Lord God of my master Abraham, if now thou do prosper my way which I go: Behold, I stand by the well of water; and it shall come to pass, that when the virgin cometh forth to draw *water,* and I say to her, Give me, I pray thee, a little water of thy pitcher to drink; And she say to me, Both drink thou, and I will also draw for thy camels: *let* the same *be* the woman whom the Lord hath appointed out for my master's son. And before I had done speaking in mine heart, behold, Rebekah came forth with her pitcher on her shoulder; and she went down unto the well, and drew *water:* and I said unto her, Let me drink, I pray thee. And she made haste, and let down her pitcher from her *shoulder,* and said, Drink, and I will give thy camels drink also: so I drank, and she made the camels drink also. And I asked her, and said, Whose daughter *art* thou? And she said, The daughter of Bethuel, Nahor's son, whom Milcah bare unto him: and I put the earring upon her face, and the bracelets upon her hands. And I bowed down my head, and worshipped the Lord, and blessed the Lord God of my master Abraham, which had led me in the right way to take my master's brother's daughter unto his son. And now if ye will deal kindly and truly with my master, tell me: and if not, tell me; that I may turn to the right hand, or to the left."[89]

Whew....For a hungry and tired man I am very impressed. This tale is orated in such a way that they will be sure of several very important things:

1. He wasn't acting on his own behalf but with the blessing of both his earthly and heavenly masters;
2. He was certain because of the behaviour and words of Rebekah that she was the one that God had led him to for his master's son; and
3. He did not want to leave empty handed. The choice was theirs of course but he fully expected them to recognise that this was the will of God and let him leave with their daughter/sister.

Now we see the outcome of this long speech. What will they decide.

"Then Laban and Bethuel answered and said, The thing proceedeth from the Lord: we cannot speak unto thee bad or good. Behold, Rebekah *is* before thee, take *her,* and go, and let her be thy master's son's wife, as the Lord hath spoken."[90]

Yay! They agreed to let him take her. The fact that this decision required no recorded discussion is significant because it shows us the character of this unnamed man. Obviously, they could tell his sincerity otherwise I doubt that they would have allowed a complete stranger, regardless of the wealth he had to offer, take their family member away just like that. She was beautiful so most likely had received at least one other offer. They could **tell** that he was a man of God and that this was the will of God.

"And it came to pass, that, when Abraham's servant heard their words, he worshipped the Lord, *bowing himself* to the earth."[91] Once again he shows his faith by acknowledging the Lord. "And the servant brought forth jewels of silver, and jewels of gold, and raiment, and gave *them* to Rebekah: he gave also to her brother and to her mother precious things. And they did eat and drink, he and the men that *were* with him, and tarried all night; and they rose up in the morning, and he said, Send me away unto my master."[92]

This man does not ever waste time. Barely recuperated from his previous journey he wants to set out for home immediately so that he can show his master that he has been successful and obedient. Now her family, probably not understanding his haste, does what any family would want to do under the circumstances - take the proper amount of time to say goodbye.

"And her brother and her mother said, Let the damsel abide with us *a few* days, at the least ten; after that she shall go." [93]

This is a legitimate request. They were about to lose their daughter/sister forever. The servant however still has his mind set on higher things and explains his reasoning.

"And he said unto them, **Hinder me not, seeing the Lord hath prospered my way**; send me away that I may go to my master."[94]

In essence what he is saying is "I know that opportunity doesn't knock very long and I don't want to show ingratitude to the Lord by failing to fulfill my duty to the letter by taking her back right away." Fair enough.

"And they said, We will call the damsel, and inquire at her mouth. And they called Rebekah, and said unto her, Wilt thou go with this man? And she said, I will go."[95]

OK now here is where I will give another shout out to Rebekah - she does not hesitate. She must have recognised that this was the will of the Lord too and was willing to act accordingly. Although her family was probably hoping that she would want to delay her departure as well they let her go and, I'm sure with tears of sorrow in their eyes, wish her Godspeed on her journey into a new life.

"And they sent away Rebekah their sister, and her nurse, and Abraham's servant, and his men. And they blessed Rebekah, and said unto her, Thou *art* our sister, be thou *the mother* of thousands of millions, and let thy seed possess the gate of those which hate them. And Rebekah arose, and her damsels, and they rode upon the camels, and followed the man: and the servant took Rebekah, and went his way."[96]

Off they go these two-faithful people. After a long journey they arrive at her new home and the servant has successfully completed his task.

"And Isaac came from the way of the well Lahai-roi; for he dwelt in the south country. And Isaac went out to meditate in the field at the eventide: and he lifted up his eyes, and saw, and, behold, the camels *were* coming. And Rebekah lifted up her eyes, and when she saw Isaac, she lighted off the camel. For she *had* said unto the servant, What man *is* this that walketh in the field to meet us? And the servant *had* said, It *is* my master: therefore she took a veil, and covered herself. **And the servant told Isaac all things that he had done.** And Isaac brought her into his mother Sarah's tent, and took Rebekah, and she became his wife; and he loved her: and Isaac was comforted after his mother's *death.*"[97]

UNLIKELY RIGHTEOUSNESS: UNSUNG HEROES OF GENESIS

I don't know if you have guessed by now but I love this man and look forward to meeting him one day! What can this unnamed spiritual giant teach us?

1. We are constantly moving towards our own future.

This servant may not have realised during all his years with Abraham the important role that he was one day going to play not only in Abraham and Isaac's lives but also in the destiny of the entire human race. Most likely he just plodded along, lovingly serving his masters and developing his faith in God - day after day after day. Had he ever been entrusted with a major assignment before? Most likely. Had he made mistakes along the way? Most likely. Did he quit and give up? No and look where it got him! He played a significant role in setting up one of the most important couples in history. May we all be ready when our definitive moments arrive.

2. Anonymity does not have to mean insignificance.

There have been many people over the millenniums who have performed faithful, anonymous acts of service who will never be acknowledged until everything is revealed at the final judgment. This man may be unnamed but he is not insignificant. His actions have benefited mankind forever and his example can inspire us several thousand years after his death even though we do not know what to call him. The neatest thing is that he didn't want the credit. Instead, he gave it all to the Lord and that makes him all the more admirable.

3. Learn the proper way to pray to get results.

This man is an excellent example for us on how to pray to get results.

- First of all he knew that his journey was in accordance with God's will and so was able to confidently ask him for his help.
- Secondly, he didn't give a "please help me in any way you see fit", wishy washy type of prayer but instead gave a very specific, "no way I can misinterpret your will" type of prayer that he would then be able to act on.
- Third, when he did receive the results he was seeking for he did not hesitate in any of his actions, even putting his own comfort behind his mission's success. This showed gratitude in both word and deed.

Like many people I have had my moments where I have sought for revelation in my prayers and have not had the type of result that I was hoping for. I hope that as I continue to study this great servant of God, and other wonderful examples of successful prayers in the scriptures, that I will be able to leave those experiences behind me in the future.

Laban - Formally Righteous Businessman

Laban is another one of those controversial characters found in the scriptures whose actions can be taken in many different ways. For those of you who did not read the previous chapter allow me to introduce you to him. Laban is Rebekah's brother making him the brother-in-law of the second patriarch of the Old Testament, Isaac. When we first meet him in Genesis 24, he appears to be still living at home with his parents, or at the very least nearby, so he may have been an unmarried young adult at that time. Many of his actions lead me to believe that in his younger years he was a good man and a spiritual person. I know this because of the things he does when Abraham's servant comes and requests Rebekah's hand in marriage (see Genesis 24:29-60 for details). First of all Laban follows the customs of the day and shows great hospitality to the servant. Then after hearing the servant's story, from both Rebekah and the servant, he recognises that it is from God, has no questions or disputes, and agrees to let Rebekah go with the man. Then after his request for her to stay another 10 days so he can say goodbye properly is denied by his sister and the servant he takes her aside and, although not a prophet, prophetically tells her she will be the mother of thousands of millions. So far so good. I like this man.

Unfortunately...he doesn't continue on this road and when we meet him several decades later he has developed some very bad habits that make him far less likable. First a little background. So as we found out in the previous chapter, Abraham's servant took Rebekah and she married Isaac. After 20 years of marriage the two of them still did not have children so Isaac prayed for his wife and she eventually conceived.[98] Not only did she conceive but she had twins - Jacob and Esau. [99] Eventually the boys grew up and it became time for them to marry. Esau made bad decisions, marrying women who could have potentially turned him away from the Lord, so Isaac and Rebekah encouraged Jacob to go and find a wife from his mother's family in Padan-aram.[100] (Yes I know, there is more to the story than that but I'll let those of you who haven't heard it before discover these details for yourselves. You're welcome.)

Jacob leaves home and after a long journey makes it to his destination. While waiting by a well he inquires about his family members (remember he had never met them) and finds out that his cousin Rachel is coming with the sheep to water her flocks.[101] Now I'm sure that the romantics in the room will love this part of the story because it appears to be love at first sight for Jacob and he is smitten by her from then on. [102] Ahhh. Rachel goes and tells her father Laban that their long-lost relative has come to visit and Jacob is invited to stay with them.[103] I'm sure that Laban was happy to find out what had happened to his sister since it had been at least 60 years since he had last seen her (Genesis 26:34 says that Esau was 40 when he married some Canaanite women so Jacob had to be at least 40 when he travelled to meet Laban). After a month Laban and Jacob have a conversation that sparks the events that show us how his character has changed since he was a young man.

"And Laban said unto Jacob, Because thou *art* my brother, shouldest thou therefore serve me for nought? tell me, what *shall* thy wages be?"[104]

I don't know whether Laban knew that Jacob was there to find a wife or not. Jacob may not have shared that with him yet. What is clear is that he has figured out that Jacob is most likely going to be around for a while so he wants to have clarity in regards to their relationship. Giving him the benefit of the doubt (you'll see why I say that later) it appears that at this time he is willing to be fair and let Jacob set the terms of his employment. Most likely he had an inkling of what was coming.

"And Laban had two daughters: the name of the elder *was* Leah, and the name of the younger *was* Rachel. Leah *was* tender eyed; but Rachel *was* beautiful and well favoured. And Jacob loved Rachel; and said, I will serve thee seven years for Rachel thy younger daughter."[105]

Most likely this suggestion of Jacob wanting Rachel did not come as a complete surprise to Laban. After all the man was neither blind nor stupid. Having had a highly desirable sister and now a beautiful daughter he must have figured out that Jacob was interested in Rachel or at least suspected it. Why the various descriptions of the girls? Well one source says that it is because "[t]he Hebrew word translated as 'tender' means 'soft, delicate, or lovely.' The fact that this trait is emphasized for Leah, while Rachel is described as 'beautiful and well-favoured,' that is, beautiful in every respect, seems to suggest that Leah's eyes were her most attractive feature."[106] There you go. Leah was not necessarily unattractive but she was not **as attractive to Jacob** as her younger sister. This makes sense as it is a common thing for people to have preferences regarding who they are interested in.

Laban appears to consider this request and agrees that it is a good idea as he says "*It is* better that I give her to thee, than that I should give her to another man: abide with me."[107] OK so it sounds like Jacob is going to get what he wants.

"And Jacob served seven years for Rachel; and they seemed unto him *but* a few days, for the love he had to her."[108]

After the seven years of service are over Jacob comes to Laban and expects him to keep his word. Sadly, there was one thing that Laban neglected to tell him before they made this arrangement and it leads him to do something both creepy and wrong.

"And Jacob said unto Laban, Give *me* my wife, for my days are fulfilled, that I may go in unto her. And Laban gathered together all the men of the place, and made a feast. And it came to pass in the evening, that he took Leah his daughter, and brought her to him; and he went in unto her."[109]

What happened to Laban during those years since he said goodbye to his sister and made us like him? Why would he do this to members of his own family? While we don't know the answers to these questions, slight-of-hand magicians would be impressed by this switch-a-roo. Jacob's wedding day has finally appeared and yet he manages to end up married to the wrong woman. Somehow Laban figured it would be okay for him to try to pass his older daughter off as Jacob's bride. Well, in a way he was right because Jacob doesn't find out about the deception until the next morning. He is not happy.

"And it came to pass, that in the morning, behold, it *was* Leah: and [Jacob] said to Laban, What *is* this thou hast done unto me? did not I serve with thee for Rachel? wherefore then hast thou beguiled me?"[110]

Now where have we seen the word beguiled before? Oh yes, it was the serpent who beguiled Eve back at the beginning of Genesis wasn't it. So what does that word mean you ask? To beguile is to "deceive"[111] in a crafty, subtle, snake-like way which is exactly what Laban did to Jacob. Laban then shows us more of his snake-like character because he then goes one step further and tries to extract more work out of Jacob.

"And Laban said, It must not be so done in our country, to give the younger before the firstborn. Fulfil her week, and we will give thee this also [i.e. Rachel] for the service which thou shalt serve with me yet seven other years."[112]

Really Laban? You could have easily mentioned the custom of the older getting married before the younger **before** Jacob worked for you for seven years and now you want seven more years from him? Another thing about this scenario bothers me. Did Laban deliberately keep Leah single during those seven years, and thus possibly forfeit her happiness if she had been in love with or wanted by someone else, so that he could pull off this deception? Was it all planned or did he really think that his older daughter would be married before now and when she wasn't **then** he made the decision? Was Leah a willing accomplice or an obedient daughter? I really don't know but the man knew Jacob's weakness and used it to his advantage and that is not cool.[113]

For now Laban may have thought that the end justified the means because he gets what he wants and Jacob agreed to the new terms.

"And Jacob did so, and fulfilled her week: and [Laban] gave him Rachel his daughter to wife also."[114]

Two daughters married off and only one son-in-law to deal with for the low price of 14 years of indentured service. You have to give him credit, Laban was a shrewd - if devious - businessman. At this point Laban must have felt like he was on top of the world. Let's see how long he stays there.

Now after marrying these two women as a result of the deception of his uncle/father-in-law it would be understandable if Jacob wanted to leave wouldn't it? That appears to be the case because "Laban said unto him, I pray thee, if I have found favour in thine eyes, *tarry: for* I have learned by experience that the Lord hath blessed me for thy sake."[115] Despite appearances here is some evidence that Laban was not completely turned away from the Lord. Right here we see that he recognised that Jacob was being blessed by God and by default Laban had been receiving those blessings too. He knew that Jacob's departure would stop the flow of blessings so he propositioned him to stay. In fact he once again offered Jacob the opportunity to set the terms. "And [Laban] said, Appoint me thy wages, and I will give *it*."[116]

Now if it was me I would have simply said no and left. Surprisingly Jacob doesn't do that and instead let's Laban know that despite being deceived by him he is not a fool.

"And [Jacob] said unto [Laban], Thou knowest how I have served thee, and how thy cattle was with me. For *it was* little which thou hadst before I *came,* and it is *now* increased unto a multitude; and the Lord hath blessed thee since my coming: and now when shall I provide for mine own house also?"[117]

In essence Jacob says to him "I know that my being here and the blessings of the Lord have made you rich. You have greatly benefitted. When is it my turn?" Fair enough after all Jacob had been single when he arrived and now he was a family man. Laban obviously finds this response encouraging because they continue negotiating.

"And [Laban] said, What shall I give thee? And Jacob said, Thou shalt not give me any thing: if thou wilt do this thing for me, I will again feed *and* keep thy flock: I will pass through all thy flock to day, removing from thence all the speckled and spotted cattle, and all the brown cattle among the sheep, and the spotted and speckled among the goats: and *of such* shall be my hire. So shall my righteousness answer for me in time to come, when it shall come for my hire before thy face: every one that *is* not speckled and spotted among the goats, and brown among the sheep, that shall be counted stolen with me. And Laban said, Behold, I would it might be according to thy word."[118]

An agreement has been made and "[Laban] removed that day the he goats that were ringstraked and spotted, and all the she goats that were speckled and spotted, *and* every one that had *some* white in it, and all the brown among the sheep, and gave *them* into the hand of his sons. And he set three days' journey betwixt himself and Jacob: and Jacob fed the rest of Laban's flocks."[119] Why three days journey? I'm not really sure but it may have been to ensure that the two flocks could not accidentally interbreed. Little did Laban know that Jacob had a plan.

"And Jacob took him rods of green poplar, and of the hazel and chestnut tree; and pilled white strakes in them, and made the white appear which *was* in the rods. And he set the rods which he had pilled before the flocks in the gutters in the watering troughs when the flocks came to drink, that they should conceive when they came to drink. And the flocks conceived before the rods, and brought forth cattle ringstraked, speckled, and spotted. And Jacob did separate the lambs, and set the faces of the flocks toward the ringstraked, and all the brown in the flock of Laban; and he put his own flocks by themselves, and put them not unto Laban's cattle. And it came to pass, whensoever the stronger cattle did conceive, that Jacob laid the rods before the eyes of the cattle in the gutters, that they might conceive among the rods. But when the cattle were feeble, he put *them* not in: so the feebler were Laban's, and the stronger Jacob's. And the man increased exceedingly, and had much cattle, and maidservants, and menservants, and camels, and asses."[120]

Whew. That was a long explanation so here is a brief summary. The separate flocks were not bred equally. Using sound animal husbandry, Jacob would breed the animals in such a way that he would ultimately end up with a large number of the stronger ones while Laban would end up with fewer, less desirable animals. The other factor in this scenario that should be remembered is that, despite Jacob's faults, the Lord blessed him because he was being obedient to the commandments. These things combined allowed him to become a very wealthy man.

Six years later "[Jacob] heard the words of Laban's sons, saying, Jacob hath taken away all that *was* our father's; and of *that* which *was* our father's hath he gotten all this glory. And Jacob beheld the countenance of Laban, and, behold, it *was* not toward him as before."[121] Gee. What a surprise that Laban and his sons are upset that Jacob has received most of the blessings and has greater flocks than they do. Knowing that he has worn out his welcome, and desiring to obey the commandment he received from God by returning to his homeland, Jacob gathers both his wives for a council and the three of them decide that it is time to leave.[122] Our little family consisting of Jacob, Rachel, Leah, their maidservants, their children and all that they possess began the long journey back home without telling Laban.[123]

One thing that Jacob didn't count on was that Laban would not only be angry at him for failing to let him know they were leaving - which was a legitimate thing to be angry about - but Rachel took her father's images which did not belong to her.[124]

"And it was told Laban on the third day that Jacob was fled. And he took his brethren with him, and pursued after him seven days' journey; and they overtook him in the mount Gilead."[125] Now angry chase scenes have played out in many stories, plays, and movies. Usually there is a heated argument once the person running is caught followed by plenty of violence. Fortunately, that wasn't the case in this one because God once again intervened giving Laban a choice.

"And God came to Laban the Syrian in a dream by night, and said unto him, Take heed that thou speak not to Jacob either good or bad."[126]

What is the choice Laban now has you may say? Well, he can do one of two things following this dream. Either he can continue with whatever he intended to do to Jacob once he caught him or he can rationally confront Jacob and form a truce. What will he decide?

"Then Laban overtook Jacob. Now Jacob had pitched his tent in the mount: and Laban with his brethren pitched in the mount of Gilead. And Laban said to Jacob, What hast thou done, that thou hast stolen away unawares to me, and carried away my daughters, as captives *taken* with the sword? Wherefore didst thou flee away secretly, and steal away from me; and didst not tell me, that I might have sent thee away with mirth, and with songs, with tabret, and with harp? And hast not suffered me to kiss my sons and my daughters? thou hast now done foolishly in *so* doing."[127]

In addition to our knowledge that Laban was a righteous man in his youth, this little speech is one of the reasons that he is in this book. Although he had mistreated his nephew/

son-in-law and his daughters what he says here lets us know that he did love his family even though he didn't always show it. Based on what he just said chances are good that he would have let them leave if they had told him that was what they were going to do. Now listen to what else he says and I will show you another reason why he is in this book.

And Laban said "It is in the power of my hand to do you hurt: but **the God of your father spake unto me** yesternight, saying, Take thou heed that thou speak not to Jacob either good or bad. And now, *though* thou wouldest needs be gone, because thou sore longedst after thy father's house, *yet* wherefore hast thou stolen my gods?"[128]

Despite the fact that some of his actions have caused Laban to turn away from God (after all he called him "the God of your father") he still respects His authority and is willing to listen to Him. He did not attack Jacob either verbally or physically but instead asked him for an explanation.

"And Jacob answered and said to Laban, Because I was afraid: for I said, Peradventure thou wouldest take by force thy daughters from me. With whomsoever thou findest thy gods, let him not live: before our brethren discern thou what *is* thine with me, and take *it* to thee. For Jacob knew not that Rachel had stolen them."[129]

Based on Laban's treatment of him you really can't blame Jacob from thinking that. Whatever the "gods" or "images" that Rachel stole were (I've read conflicting interpretations of that) they were obviously very important to him because he "... went into Jacob's tent, and into Leah's tent, and into the two maidservants' tents; but he found *them* not. Then went he out of Leah's tent, and entered into Rachel's tent. Now Rachel had taken the images, and put them in the camel's furniture, and sat upon them. And Laban searched all the tent, but found *them* not. And she said to her father, Let it not displease my lord that I cannot rise up before thee; for the custom of women *is* upon me. And he searched, but found not the images."[130]

Not locating his property after searching everywhere for it must have been pretty embarrassing for Laban, especially now that he has to face Jacob after accusing him outright. Jacob does not mince words.

"And Jacob was wroth, and chode with Laban: and Jacob answered and said to Laban, What *is* my trespass? what *is* my sin, that thou hast so hotly pursued after me? Whereas thou hast searched all my stuff, what hast thou found of all thy household stuff? set *it* here before my brethren and thy brethren, that they may judge betwixt us both. This twenty years *have* I *been* with thee; thy ewes and thy she goats have not cast their young, and the rams of thy flock have I not eaten. That which was torn *of beasts* I brought not unto thee; I bare the loss of it; of my hand didst thou require it, *whether* stolen by day, or stolen by night. *Thus* I was; in the day the drought consumed me, and the frost by night; and my sleep departed from mine eyes. Thus have I been twenty years in thy house; I served thee fourteen years for thy two daughters, and six years for thy cattle: and thou hast changed my wages ten times. Except the God of my father, the God of Abraham, and the fear of Isaac, had been with me, surely thou hadst sent me away now empty. God hath seen mine affliction and the labour of my hands, and rebuked *thee* yesternight."[131]

Despite his frustration, and most likely very red face, Laban does not back down. You have to give him credit for courage and also for once again showing that he did love his family because he makes Jacob promise that he will treat them properly.

"And Laban answered and said unto Jacob, *These* **daughters** *are* **my daughters, and** *these* **children** *are* **my children,** and *these* cattle *are* my cattle, and all that thou seest *is* mine: and what can I do this day unto these my daughters, or unto their children which they have born? Now therefore come thou, let us make a covenant, I and thou; and let it be for a witness between me and thee. And Jacob took a stone, and set it up *for* a pillar. And Jacob said unto his brethren, Gather stones; and they took stones, and made an heap: and they did eat there upon the heap. And Laban called it Jegar-sahadutha: but Jacob called it Galeed. And Laban said, This heap *is* a witness between me and thee this day. Therefore was the name of it called Galeed; And Mizpah; for he said, The Lord watch between me and thee, when we are absent one from another. **If thou shalt afflict my daughters, or if thou shalt take** *other* **wives beside my daughters, no man** *is* **with us; see, God** *is* **witness betwixt me and thee.** And Laban said to Jacob, Behold this heap, and behold *this* pillar, which I have cast betwixt me and thee; This heap *be* witness, and *this* pillar *be* witness, that I will not pass over this heap to thee, and that thou shalt not pass over this heap and this pillar unto me, for harm. **The God of Abraham, and the God of Nahor, the God of their father, judge betwixt us.** And Jacob sware by the fear of his father Isaac."[132]</p>

Laban loved his family. While he did not follow God anymore, he knew that Jacob did and used that relationship to ensure that he would not ever break their covenant. The two men are done with each other.

"Then Jacob offered sacrifice upon the mount, and called his brethren to eat bread: and they did eat bread, and tarried all night in the mount. And early in the morning Laban rose up, and kissed his sons and his daughters, and blessed them: and Laban departed, and returned unto his place."[133]

Despite the fact that I do not now or ever will agree with many of the things that Laban did and said I do feel for him at this moment. Several decades earlier he lost his sister and never saw her again and now, while he will still have his sons and possibly unnamed daughters around him, he will lose contact with two of his daughters and his grandchildren. He also must realise that unless he repents he will never again have the favor and blessings of the Lord. He leaves a broken man and we never hear from him in the Bible again. How sad.

What can Laban teach us?

1. Diligence is key to maintaining any relationship.

I really do think that Laban was spiritual in his youth but he had lost most of that spirituality by the time his nephew met him. Righteousness is not a given - it requires constantly making good decisions, repenting when necessary, and trying to align your life with what the Lord would want you to do and have. We have nothing to go on regarding what happened to him in the intervening years. No anecdotes are given, no stories are told, he says nothing so we don't know if his turning away was gradual or dramatic. What we do know is that had he stayed strong and built his relationship with God instead of turning away from him he may have been more successful, and may have been an inspiration to his children and grandchildren, instead of becoming a liar and a deceiver and knowing that the last time they were together his daughters were not sad to see him go. He also had the final recorded message given to him by the Lord as being a warning laced with disappointment of an "I'm proud of you my son" message.

2. Success built on deceit is temporary.

At one stage in this story Laban may have felt that he had it all - a blessed son in-law, free labour, his family around him, and increased flocks. Unfortunately, due to the law of the harvest, which states that you reap what you sow, he did not keep it. The Lord blessed Jacob and Laban lost the majority of his flocks. His daughters hated him and would have told their children the story of how the two of them ended up married to Jacob - after all Leah may not have ended up as Jacob's wife by choice - which would have made them think less of their grandfather. Most importantly, he lost the relationship he had with God and although unlike Cain we don't hear him lament it - he had to miss it slightly. In the end he was left with nothing that lasts - except for the reputation of a scoundrel. It is my hope that he has repented since.

3. Those that trust in God are protected and blessed.

We have no way of knowing what Laban had intended to do to Jacob when he caught up with him before the warning he received in the dream from God. That he was warned shows us that God protects his servants from harm. Not only were Jacob and his family protected but Laban was also protected because he was prevented from doing something that would potentially have led to permanent spiritual harm.

Leah - The Other Woman

Leah is a woman who I think was more important to the story of the Children of Israel than we tend to give her credit for. Unfortunately, like most of the people mentioned so far, we have to speculate and fill in the blanks in order to tell her story because the Bible is IRITATINGLY SILENT on the subject. When we first meet her she is described by the author of Genesis almost as an afterthought.

"And Laban had two daughters: the name of the elder *was* Leah, and the name of the younger *was* Rachel. Leah *was* tender eyed; but Rachel *was* beautiful and well favoured."[134]

That's it? That's all you have to say about her? At least we know from the story that Rachel was a shepherdess but the Bible is silent about Leah other than to tell us that her eyes were her best feature. What did she like to do and to have? What role did she play in this story? How old was she when the story took place? After all we know that she was older than Rachel, and that Laban had at least two sons, but we don't know if she was the oldest or somewhere in the middle. As a result of this scriptural silence I would like to put the disclaimer out there that although I have had to do a lot of speculation in order to tell her story I have tried to ask myself enough questions that I can be as accurate as possible so that I can pay her the honour that I feel she deserves.

Now back to her story. Despite what we don't know about Leah, we do know that she was single when her cousin Jacob came to live with them and fell in love with her sister Rachel. For those of you who remember the story in the previous chapter, Leah ends up becoming Jacob's first wife due to her father's tricking him into marrying the wrong woman. One of the things that we must assume for THAT scenario to make sense is that Leah had remained single throughout the seven years that Jacob worked for Rachel.

We can infer this for two reasons:

1. Laban uses the excuse that Leah the older must be married before he can marry off his younger daughter in order to justify his tricking of Jacob,

2. as Judah in Genesis 38, the story of Ruth and Boaz, and Jesus Christ in the gospels[135] all make clear, one of the customs of the day designed to protect women was that if a man died without having children, then his brother(s) or other close male relatives were required to marry his widow to keep his name alive and ensure she had children to take care of her later on in life. Unless Leah had previously married an only child or a man with only sisters this custom would have prevented Laban from needing to trick Jacob in that manner.

UNLIKELY RIGHTEOUSNESS: UNSUNG HEROES OF GENESIS

OK so we know that through trickery Leah and her younger sister are both married to their cousin Jacob. Now let's review the situation Leah finds herself by this point in the story. We do not know what her role in becoming Jacob's wife was or if she even WANTED to marry Jacob in the first place because the first time we actually hear her speak is regarding her first-born son. Whether she was a dutiful daughter who went along with it against her will or a willing accomplice is not really clear. What we do know is that despite being the first wife she was not the preferred wife. A week after marrying Leah Jacob "went in also unto Rachel, and he loved also Rachel more than Leah, and served with [Laban] yet seven other years."[136]

If Leah's only goal in life was to get married then she has accomplished it. For the rest of her life Jacob supports her and respects her. We have no evidence that she was ever abused either mentally, physically, or verbally by her husband - either before the covenant Laban extracted from Jacob or after it - so even though the Bible makes clear that she was loved less than her sister she had a satisfactory marriage. If like many people in the western hemisphere however she had always wanted a partnership between loving spouses full of passion and romance - well then she failed horribly because Jacob had been honest with them from the start. He had always indicated that he wanted Rachel not Leah. For all we know they liked each other and had looked forward during the seven years he lived with them to being an in-laws but not spouses. They were cousins so may have felt a familial bond and developed a friendship. Unfortunately for Leah, knowing that her younger sister was loved more than she was hurt her and made her feel lonely. How to overcome this loneliness? How about adding children to the mix.

"And when the Lord saw that Leah *was* hated, he opened her womb: but Rachel *was* barren. And Leah conceived, and bare a son, and she called his name Reuben: for she said, Surely the Lord hath looked upon my affliction; **now therefore my husband will love me**. And she conceived again, and bare a son; and said, **Because the Lord hath heard that I *was* hated**, he hath therefore given me this *son* also: and she called his name Simeon. And she conceived again, and bare a son; and said, Now **this time will my husband be joined unto me**, because I have born him three sons: therefore was his name called Levi. And she conceived again, and bare a son: and she said, **Now will I praise the Lord**: therefore she called his name Judah; and left bearing."[137]

The above verses would have taken at least four years to accomplish and left Leah a young mother with four sons. Rereading this brief, and somewhat coldly stated, account makes me sad. You can hear the mental battle in her head from the things she says each time a son is born. There is joy at becoming a mother but there is also the hope that NOW Jacob will love her the same as he does Rachel. Since she keeps trying with each child you must assume that hope kept being dashed as giving him more children never changed his feelings for her. In a way this actually lets us know a bit about Jacob's character. Like his father Isaac, Jacob was emotionally and physically faithful to his wives never once losing his love for Rachel despite what she could not give him and not cutting himself off from Leah physically despite not wanting her as a spouse at first. The ideal situation for all involved - well no - but by now we are used to people in the scriptures having to deal with trials and still succeeding.

Another thing I'd like to point out is how the Lord honours Leah during all of this. What is neat to those of us living now is that we can look back and see how the sons she is given show the trust the Lord must have had in her. For example Moses - one of the greatest prophets who ever lived; his brother Aaron - who with his sons became the first priests of the house of Israel to serve in the tabernacle; and John the Baptist - the forerunner of the Saviour Jesus Christ were all descendants of Levi.[138] Leah's son Judah played an even more important role since it was through his line that two of the greatest kings of Israel, David and Solomon, and the Saviour Jesus Christ came[139]. Leah, not Rachel, was the one blessed to be the ancestress of these great men. After her fourth son is born she stops having children for a while.

Meanwhile Rachel watched her sister succeed with envy and decided that she would not be outdone so, taking a page out of Sarah's book, she gives her handmaiden Bilhah to Jacob so that she can adopt their children.[140] Like Abraham Jacob goes along with it and he and Bilhah have two sons, Dan and Naphtali, which Rachel then adopts as her own.[141] The score is now four natural born children for Leah and two adopted children for Rachel. Despite the fact that she is still ahead number wise Leah must have felt that she wasn't done having children. For reasons that are not stated, she was not able to do that herself so she also gives her handmaiden Zilpah to Jacob and has two more adopted sons, Gad and Asher, through her.[142] These two rivalling sisters are now up to: Leah - six children (four natural and two adopted) and Rachel - two adopted children.

One has to wonder how much contact they had with each other's families during all of these years. They did not live in cities with millions of people where it is easy to avoid each other after all. Did Rachel help Leah take care of her children? Did Leah help Bilhah with her two children? Was Rachel there helping her sister each time she gave birth? If so then that may have been a bonding moment for the two of them even if only temporarily. What is especially sad so far is that they were sisters and instead of supporting each other through their various trials they were competing with one another. Rachel's competitive spirit and/or desperation to have children of her own ultimately lead to another victory for Leah on the children front at least.

"And Reuben went in the days of wheat harvest, and found mandrakes in the field, and brought them unto his mother Leah. Then Rachel said to Leah, Give me, I pray thee, of thy son's mandrakes. And she said unto her, **Is it a small matter that thou hast taken my husband? and wouldest thou take away my son's mandrakes also?** And Rachel said, Therefore he shall lie with thee to night for thy son's mandrakes. And Jacob came out of the field in the evening, and Leah went out to meet him, and said, Thou must come in unto me; for surely I have hired thee with my son's mandrakes. And he lay with her that night. And God hearkened unto Leah, and she conceived, and bare Jacob the fifth son. And Leah said, **God hath given me my hire, because I have given my maiden to my husband:** and she called his name Issachar. And Leah conceived again,

and bare Jacob the sixth son. And Leah said, **God hath endued
me *with* a good dowry; now will my husband dwell with
me**, because I have born him six sons: and she called his name
Zebulun. And afterwards she bare a daughter, and called her
name Dinah."[143]

Here we get to see how lonely each sister really was. Leah
was surrounded by children but still wanted what her sister had
- the love of her husband. Rachel had the love of her husband
but longed to bear a child - something her sister had no trouble
doing. In the bargain that they struck here Leah is the winner
because she has three more children. While this bargain didn't
immediately help Rachel out, she does eventually have her first
son - Joseph.[144]

Now the scriptures tell us that after marrying Leah and
Rachel, Jacob had worked for Laban for an additional 13 years
(seven to pay for Rachel's dowry and six to build up his own
wealth). After this time Jacob feels it is time to leave and we
see that despite loving Rachel more than Leah, when it came to
family decisions he treated them equally because he calls **both**
of his wives to him so that they can **discuss** their next move.
They were not second-class citizens in his eyes nor was he a
dictator.

"And Jacob sent and called Rachel and Leah to the field
unto his flock, And said unto them, I see your father's
countenance, that it *is* not toward me as before; but the God
of my father hath been with me. And ye know that with all my
power I have served your father. And your father hath deceived
me, and changed my wages ten times; but God suffered him
not to hurt me. If he said thus, The speckled shall be thy wages;

then all the cattle bare speckled: and if he said thus, The ringstraked shall be thy hire; then bare all the cattle ringstraked. Thus God hath taken away the cattle of your father, and given *them* to me. And it came to pass at the time that the cattle conceived, that I lifted up mine eyes, and saw in a dream, and, behold, the rams which leaped upon the cattle *were* ringstraked, speckled, and grisled. And the angel of God spake unto me in a dream, *saying,* Jacob: And I said, Here *am* I. And he said, Lift up now thine eyes, and see, all the rams which leap upon the cattle *are* ringstraked, speckled, and grisled: for I have seen all that Laban doeth unto thee. I *am* the God of Beth-el, where thou anointedst the pillar, *and* where thou vowedst a vow unto me: now arise, get thee out from this land, and return unto the land of thy kindred."[145]

Jacob has restated information that the girls already knew since they had participated in this drama with their father along with him. The conversation is interesting because despite their rivalry when it came to children and the love of their husband the sisters are united on this topic. They do not show any loyalty towards their father because not only had he tricked Jacob into marrying both of them (which we still don't know if Leah had wanted him in the beginning or not) but he had also tried to cheat him again over the years AND had also mistreated the two of them.

"And Rachel and Leah answered and said unto [Jacob], *Is there* yet any portion or inheritance for us in our father's house? Are we not counted of him strangers? for he hath sold us, and hath quite devoured also our money. For all the riches which God hath taken from our father, that *is* ours, and our children's: now then, **whatsoever God hath said unto thee**, do."[146]

What is interesting about this is they did not only want to leave for practical reasons. True they felt estranged from their father and saw that no inheritance was coming but they also show their own faith in God because they encourage their husband to be obedient to the commandment he had received. One can only guess what information that Jacob had shared with each of them over the years from his interactions with God or all of the spiritual experiences that they themselves had. Many times when Leah had given birth she mentions her gratitude for God but right here she and Rachel are both putting their money where their mouth is because this will be a major change. They will be leaving their homeland, neighbours, kindred, and everything familiar to them forever and travelling to a place they have only heard of but never been to. That will take courage and faith.

OK now for the move. Now this would have been a major undertaking because they had to not only move their possessions but their homes as well since they lived in tents. All of this would have been done with animals, carts, and on foot. Now for those of you who read the previous chapter you know that after three days journey Laban finds out they've left and chases them down. He searches the camp for the images that Rachel stole, doesn't find them, and makes Jacob promise not to ever marry other women or mistreat his wives. He leaves and they never see him again. We don't know how aware Leah and Rachel's children were of what their grandfather had done to their mothers and father. One of the most inspiring women I met while on a mission was in the process of going through a divorce. Despite the fact that we could tell from the things she said that it was somewhat messy I cannot remember her ever saying anything derogatory or insulting about her ex-husband. Even if Leah had taken this same road with her children, never once putting Laban down in front of them or speaking in a disrespectful tone to him, they would have been able to read between the lines and would have known that she was not happy with her father which may have affected their relationship with him.

During their journey to their final home several events occur that must have had a significant effect on Leah's life and may even have tested her faith in God. First, they receive word that Jacob's brother Esau, who had wanted to kill him the last time they were together, is on his way to meet them with four hundred men.[147] Things work out okay but there was a lot of fear first (see the next chapter for details). Then while they are camping near Shechem her daughter Dinah is kidnapped, raped, and held against her will until two of Leah's sons, Simeon and Levi, go and retrieve her becoming murderers and deceivers in the process.[148] Then an undisclosed amount of time later her sister Rachel dies in childbirth.[149] That last event must have been especially hard for her to deal with. She had already had to deal with the pain of watching her daughter become the victim of a crime and her sons become criminals and now her sister, the only remaining blood relative she has from her youth, is dead. Despite their rivalry over Jacob - I'd like to think that the sisters did love each other and Leah may really have missed Rachel once she was gone.

Leah now has a new situation to deal with. As Jacob's remaining wife she would most likely have been the woman responsible for helping raise her nephews Joseph and Benjamin. Benjamin never knew his mother but Joseph did and, while we don't know for certain how old he was when she died, he had to be quite young since he was the last born before they set out for Jacob's home country. This would mean that Leah would have the responsibility for ensuring they were raised properly. A responsibility that she was probably keenly aware of after Levi and Simeon's actions earlier in the story. I wonder if during this short reprieve from tragedy she now felt that things were only going to get better. Not so because for reasons that are not stated, while they are camping "beyond the tower of Edar"[150] Jacob and Leah's first-born son Reuben "went and lay with Bilhah his father's concubine: and Israel [aka Jacob] heard *it*."[151] I don't know if he raped her or if he seduced her but either way Reuben's action violated the law of chastity and dishonoured both his father and his mother. Now for several chapters we have seen her dealing with loss, fear, and pain but we don't have any mention of how she was handling it. In a way that is good **because** other women in the scriptures, such as David's wife Michal[152], who criticised him for the way he chose to worship the Lord, and Job's unnamed wife[153], who encouraged him to abandon his faith and give up, are notorious for their less than encouraging words to their husbands during important moments in their lives. As no such comments are recorded for Leah we must assume that while she was probably heart broken by this time she had not lost her faith. Perhaps, even though it is not recorded, she had her own grand spiritual experience with God that gave her the strength to keep going no matter what.

The next event in Leah's life is one that her sister never got to experience. She meets Isaac, the second patriarch in their family, a prophet of God, and her father in-law.

"And Jacob came unto Isaac his father unto Mamre, unto the city of Arbah, which *is* Hebron, where Abraham and Isaac sojourned. And the days of Isaac were an hundred and fourscore years. And Isaac gave up the ghost, and died, and was gathered unto his people, *being* old and full of days: and his sons Esau and Jacob buried him."[154]

What that experience was like for her, what Isaac may have said to her, and how long he stayed alive once they joined him again is anyone's guess. I think that she probably recognised the honour of being the woman that Jacob brought home and also how honoured Isaac was by the Lord that he had lived to see his sons reconciled and witness the results of letting his son Jacob go all those years ago. Isaac was able to meet all of his grandchildren before he died. Sadly, for Jacob, the fact that Rebekah is not mentioned at all here leads me to believe that she did not live to see her sons reconciled or Jacob return home.

By this point in the story, I am assuming that Leah is still alive because no mention of her death has been recorded. If so, then fortunately for Leah, that reprieve that she hadn't gotten earlier occurs because we have nothing major recorded for several years - no deaths, no births, no lies, no fights, no famines, nothing. Unfortunately, it seems that the good times can't last forever and, several years later, a new family conflict occurs. Remember her nephew Joseph? Well now he is a young man and is acting as a foreman for his father.

"And Jacob dwelt in the land wherein his father was a stranger, in the land of Canaan. These *are* the generations of Jacob. Joseph, *being* seventeen years old, was feeding the flock with his brethren; and the lad *was* with the sons of Bilhah, and with the sons of Zilpah, his father's wives: and Joseph brought unto his father their evil report."[155]

Okay so the text tells us that Joseph was the favored son but he was also one of the youngest sons so the fact that he is in charge shows us that he was also trustworthy and hardworking. Tattling on his half brothers, while part of his duties, would not have made them his friends. Then Jacob does something that will change this family forever.

"Now Israel loved Joseph more than all his children, because he *was* the son of his old age: and he made him a coat of *many* colours. And when his brethren saw that their father loved him more than all his brethren, they hated him, and could not speak peaceably unto him."[156]

Okay so tensions in their camp were probably already high because Joseph had ratted out his brothers but now they are past the point of no return - the ten sons hated Joseph. I wonder what this situation was like for Leah. I do not know for sure what influence she may have had on Joseph, after a certain age Jacob could have been more of a care giver to him than she was, but after watching him grow up and having him and Benjamin as the only tangible reminders that she had of her sister she may truly have loved him as a son rather than a nephew. Depending on her own level of faith what happened next may have either strengthened her testimony of God or weakened it.

"And Joseph dreamed a dream, and he told *it* his brethren: and they hated him yet the more. And he said unto them, Hear, I pray you, this dream which I have dreamed: For, behold, we *were* binding sheaves in the field, and, lo, my sheaf arose, and also stood upright; and, behold, your sheaves stood round about, and made obeisance to my sheaf. And his brethren said to him, Shalt thou indeed reign over us? or shalt thou indeed have dominion over us? And they hated him yet the more for his dreams, and for his words. And he dreamed yet another dream, and told it his brethren, and said, Behold, I have dreamed a dream more; and, behold, the sun and the moon and the eleven stars made obeisance to me. And he told *it* to his father, and to his brethren: and his father rebuked him, and said unto him, What *is* this dream that thou hast dreamed? Shall I and thy mother and thy brethren indeed come to bow down ourselves to thee to the earth? And his brethren envied him; but his father observed the saying."[157]

These were not just dreams. Jacob's reaction shows us that he understood that they were prophetic in nature showing Joseph and his family what would happen in the future. Leah's reaction to these dreams is again not given however I am sure she heard them because we still have nothing recorded regarding her death until the end of Genesis. Sadly, if she was still alive by this point she had one more tragedy to go through. Her sons, Bilhah's sons, and Zilpah's sons went to feed their flocks in Shechem and Joseph was sent to see how they were doing. He never came back. We know because we have the records that his brothers attacked him and sold him into slavery but the story they told their father was that he had been killed by a wild beast which absolutely devastated Jacob.[158] Even if she had not loved Joseph herself seeing the reaction of her husband would have caused her empathy and womanly instincts to kick in. How many tears did she shed? I don't know. How fervent were her prayers for her husband and family during this time of mourning? I don't know. Did she even suspect that her sons were lying? Sorry, no idea.

The next time we hear Leah's name it is when Jacob is in Egypt and is preparing to die. He tells his sons that he wants to be buried in the family crypt, a cave that Abraham had bought several years earlier in Canaan, where Jacob had also buried Leah.[159] When she died is not indicated but she did not make it to Egypt with them. As a result, she was not able to see what great things her nephew/adopted son had accomplished since he left them over twenty years earlier. Because the writers of Genesis chose to focus on Joseph's story during those years only God knows the rest of the story of this enigmatic woman.

Lessons from Leah's story:

1) Parents are not always right.

Laban was wrong to trick Jacob into marrying Leah and Leah was wrong to go along with it. One of the truths of the Gospel of Jesus Christ is that no one - not a parent, spouse, child, friend, acquaintance, or government official - has the right or ability to make you do something that is wrong. I don't know what her role in getting married was but this may have been one of the instances where disobeying your parents may have been justified. True through the grace of God Leah, Jacob, and Rachel were all blessed, making lemonade out of their situation, but one can't help but wonder how much happier her life may have been if her father had not chosen to deceive Jacob in this manner.

2. God will bless your future.

As mentioned earlier Leah had the honour of being the ancestress of some of the most significant and famous men in history. Her role was also to be the mother of half of the tribes that eventually became what we know as the Children of Israel. She had numerous descendents, at least some spiritual experiences that helped build her faith, and the chance to meet her father-in-law. She also lived long enough to "grow old" with Jacob and they may truly have loved each other by the time she died. If nothing else she is given the honour of being buried with the patriarchs showing the respect that her husband had for her when she died. These things were not insignificant and hopefully she appreciated the blessings she did receive even though her life probably did not end up the way she would have wanted it to.

3. Life will throw you curve balls.

Despite what some people will tell you no one can predict the future. Even prophets do not always know **exactly** how or when the revelations that they receive from God will happen.

UNLIKELY RIGHTEOUSNESS: UNSUNG HEROES OF GENESIS

Look at Joseph who knew through his dreams that his future was going to be great but could not have predicted that he would be a slave before that would happen. Leah had many trials thrown her way that could have completely bowled over a weaker woman. Her children disappointed her or were victims, her father mistreated her, she did not feel sufficiently loved by her husband, she may have witnessed the horrible death of her sister, she suffered many losses, and she never found out what happened to Joseph. Despite it all she remained strong and we can follow her example in that regard even if we don't know every step she took along her journey.

Esau - Also Blessed

The relationship between Esau and his brother Jacob was complicated right from the womb. Literally. After twenty years of marriage their parents Isaac and Rebekah were suffering from the family problem - infertility. Now these parents had great faith and great relationships with God and they used that faith to overcome this problem.

"And Isaac **entreated** the Lord for his wife, because she *was* barren: and the Lord was entreated of him, and Rebekah his wife conceived."[160]

These children were miracle children but right from the beginning they were not getting along.

"And the children struggled together within her; and she said, If *it be* so, why *am* I thus? And she went to inquire of the Lord."[161]

We don't know what experience that Rebekah had with pregnant women. Although they had not had children up to this point this may not have been her first pregnancy - she may have miscarried before. What we can infer is that she was smart or educated enough to recognise that the symptoms she was experiencing were not normal. She makes an interesting choice here because instead of getting her husband to inquire of the

Lord for her, as she could have done because he was a prophet, she does it herself and has her own great spiritual experience as a result.

"And the Lord said unto her, Two nations *are* in thy womb, and two manner of people shall be separated from thy bowels; and *the one* people shall be stronger than *the other* people; and the elder shall serve the younger."[162]

Something about this verse makes me think that we do not have the full story. In my experience the Lord is willing to spend as much time with you as you need when you come to him in prayer so I doubt that this was the entire conversation that the two of them had. Again, the rest of the information she received may have been too sacred for us to have so the writers of Genesis were only allowed to record the information that **we** would need to be able to understand the rest of the story. Sure enough when her sons are born they are as physically different as two brother can possibly be. As they grew older their differences became more apparent.

"And when her days to be delivered were fulfilled, behold, *there were* twins in her womb. And the first came out red, all over like an hairy garment; and they called his name Esau. And after that came his brother out, and his hand took hold on Esau's heel; and his name was called Jacob: and Isaac *was* threescore years old when she bare them. And the boys grew: and Esau was a cunning hunter, a man of the field; and Jacob *was* a plain man, dwelling intents."[163]

Now the next few verses are essential for us to understand a few things about the family situation that was playing itself out here.

First of all, we learn that while both parents probably loved both their children they did have their favorites. "And Isaac loved Esau, because he did eat of *his* venison: but Rebekah loved Jacob."[164] Why Rebekah loved Jacob is a mystery although it could have been because she felt sorry for him since he wasn't favoured by his father. It could also be that he was easier to raise than Esau or maybe she felt a need to tutor him more after the revelation that she had received while pregnant. Now we get to the part of the story which has been the most controversial over the years because it makes us wonder if God is really fair in how He deals with His children.

"And Jacob sod pottage: and Esau came from the field, and he *was* faint: And Esau said to Jacob, Feed me, I pray thee, with that same red *pottage;* for I *am* faint: therefore was his name called Edom. And Jacob said, Sell me this day thy birthright. And Esau said, Behold, I *am* at the point to die: and **what profit shall this birthright do to me?** And Jacob said, Swear to me this day; and he sware unto him: and he sold his birthright unto Jacob. Then Jacob gave Esau bread and pottage of lentiles; and he did eat and drink, and rose up, and went his way: **thus Esau despised *his* birthright**."[165]

This conversation comes across as wrong on many levels to us in modern day. First of all, how can we possibly consider Jacob as being a man of God when he would be willing to take advantage of his own brother during his time of weakness? Second, what right did Jacob have asking for the birthright in the first place when as far as scholars have led us to understand these things were strictly dealt with through the social customs of the day. Had his mother shared with him the information she received from God while she was pregnant and that prompted him to make this suggestion? Third, how much did Esau really understand about his birthright and how much did he value it? When he was finished eating it says he "despised" it but I wonder if that was because he no longer had it or did he look down on it before as well by taking it for granted?

OK so let's see what the experts have said that can maybe give us some insight. Referring to the fact that Esau seemed to think he was going to die from hunger one source has said: "This rationalization seems to reflect more scorn than hunger. Jacob would almost certainly have succored Esau freely if his life were in jeopardy. The point of this account seems to be primarily to show how little value Esau placed on the birthright. His immediate bodily needs were more important to him than the rights of the covenant. Additional evidence of this attitude is Esau's marriages to Canaanite women, which broke the covenant line (see Genesis 26:34–35[1]). The birthright itself should have been a treasured thing. The highly desirable birthright blessing is the right to the presidency, or keys, of the priesthood."[166] From this statement and the effort previous generations in this family had made to keep the line pure it looks as if Esau didn't get the eternal significance of the birthright he as the oldest held. If he had then he would have made better decisions in his life so that his upcoming "death" from hunger would not have frightened him because no one could have taken those blessings from him. Sadly, by choosing to marry outside of the covenant and to not keep an

---

1.   https://www.lds.org/scriptures/ot/gen/

26.34-35?lang=eng#a5c02393e59c943d6a75a9241140faca333

eternal perspective he had already lost the spiritual blessings. All Jacob took from him was the tangible blessings that Esau wouldn't have been able to take with him anyway when he died.

Now let's talk about Jacob. Did he truly understand what he was doing? I'm not sure. These two brothers had been at odds since the womb so we don't know how close they were to each other. Maybe this wasn't the first time Esau had come in from the field demanding food and not shown consideration or gratitude for it. Maybe Jacob had had enough of this behaviour and decided to say something to Esau designed to see if he recognised that even though Jacob wasn't a hunter he still worked hard and wanted to be appreciated. Regardless of Jacob's motives he and the Lord were not done with Esau. The next event in his life also seems grossly unfair until you look at it in the right context.

"And it came to pass, that when Isaac was old, and his eyes were dim, so that he could not see, he called Esau his eldest son, and said unto him, My son: and he said unto him, Behold, *here am* I. And he said, Behold now, I am old, I know not the day of my death: Now therefore take, I pray thee, thy weapons, thy quiver and thy bow, and go out to the field, and take me *some* venison; And make me savoury meat, such as I love, and bring *it* to me, that I may eat; that my soul may bless thee before I die."[167] One of the things that we learned earlier is that Isaac loved Esau because of the food that he provided for him. We can also infer from this that not only could Esau find the game but he knew how to cook it properly to bring out the best flavours. As his death approaches Isaac wants to share a final meal with Esau and give him a blessing. Little did Isaac know that his wife was going to intervene.

"And Rebekah heard when Isaac spake to Esau his son. And Esau went to the field to hunt *for* venison, *and* to bring *it*. And Rebekah spake unto Jacob her son, saying, Behold, I heard thy father speak unto Esau thy brother, saying, Bring me venison, and make me savoury meat, that I may eat, and bless thee before the Lord before my death. Now therefore, my son, obey my voice according to that which I command thee. Go now to the flock, and fetch me from thence two good kids of the goats; and I will make them savoury meat for thy father, such as he loveth: And thou shalt bring *it* to thy father, that he may eat, and that he may bless thee before his death."[168]

Rebekah's actions here have caused many people to wonder about her motivations. I know that she favoured Jacob, and that she disapproved of her daughters-in-law through Esau, but why is she trying to circumvent her husband and son here? This is just my guess but I think that Rebekah knew more than Isaac about the Lord's will in this case. As with many of the other people we meet in the scriptures who have deeply personal and sacred conversations with God we don't know if she ever shared what she learned while pregnant with Isaac or not. If she didn't then she may have been taking matters in her own hands by trying to bring about God's will in her own way instead of letting things play out as they were intended. We will never know what the alternatives could have been because this is the path she chose. To his credit, while he doesn't say "Mom this is wrong for moral reasons" Jacob does not appear to be completely comfortable with betraying his brother and father and instead tries to talk her out of it using practical reasons.

"And Jacob said to Rebekah his mother, Behold, Esau my brother *is* a hairy man, and I *am* a smooth man: My father peradventure will feel me, and I shall seem to him as a deceiver; and I shall bring a curse upon me, and not a blessing. And his mother said unto him, Upon me *be* thy curse, my son: only obey my voice, and go fetch me *them*."[169] Rebekah was a very determined woman even going so far as to say "If I am wrong about this and it does not work I will take all of the consequences upon me." We do not know if Jacob was still uncomfortable with it or not but he did as he was told. "And he went, and fetched, and brought *them* to his mother: and his mother made savoury meat, such as his father loved. And Rebekah took goodly raiment of her eldest son Esau, which *were* with her in the house, and put them upon Jacob her younger son: And she put the skins of the kids of the goats upon his hands, and upon the smooth of his neck: And she gave the savoury meat and the bread, which she had prepared, into the hand of her son Jacob."[170]

I'm not sure what was going on in Jacob's mind at this moment. Unless he had always wanted to deceive his father, and by default break the commandments of God, he was probably not very comfortable with this scenario. Nevertheless, he went forward with it.

"And he came unto his father, and said, My father: and he said, Here *am* I; who *art* thou, my son?"[171] This is the point of no return. Up to this point Jacob can still turn around. If he goes forward with this there is no turning back. "And Jacob said unto his father, I *am* Esau thy firstborn; I have done according as thou badest me: arise, I pray thee, sit and eat of my venison, that thy soul may bless me."[172]

Now from the conversation that occurs next we know that Isaac smelled a rat. He may not have been able to see that it was Jacob but he could hear the differences in his son's voices. He was suspicious and decided to make sure he knew who he was talking to.

"And Isaac said unto his son, How *is it* that thou hast found *it* so quickly, my son? And [Jacob] said, Because the Lord thy God brought *it* to me. And Isaac said unto Jacob, Come near, I pray thee, that I may feel thee, my son, whether thou *be* my very son Esau or not. And Jacob went near unto Isaac his father; and he felt him, and said, The voice *is* Jacob's voice, but the hands *are* the hands of Esau. **And he discerned him not**, because his hands were hairy, as his brother Esau's hands: **so he blessed him**."[173]

Isaac was old and although he had been careful up to this point he was still human and capable of making mistakes. Aside from his sense of hearing he also used his senses of smell and feel to discern who he was talking to. Unfortunately, they failed him in this regard and he could not tell that it is Jacob not Esau he is talking to because of the disguise Jacob was wearing. One thing I wonder is why didn't Isaac just ask God who he was talking to? No matter how good our disguise we cannot fool God. If he did either God didn't answer him or it wasn't recorded.

UNLIKELY RIGHTEOUSNESS: UNSUNG HEROES OF GENESIS

"And [Isaac] said, *Art* thou my very son Esau? And [Jacob] said, I *am.* And [Isaac] said, Bring *it* near to me, and I will eat of my son's venison, that my soul may bless thee. And [Jacob] brought *it* near to him, and he did eat: and he brought him wine, and he drank. And his father Isaac said unto him, Come near now, and kiss me, my son. And he came near, and kissed him: and he smelled the smell of his raiment, and blessed him, and said, See, the smell of my son *is* as the smell of a field which the Lord hath blessed:"[174]

Now before we move on I want to explain something for those of you who may not be LDS so that you can better understand my perspective on this situation. When giving this blessing to his son Isaac may not have been acting completely on his own regard. Prophets of God, as Isaac was, are given something called the priesthood which is "the authority and power that God gives to man to act in the name of Jesus Christ in all things for the salvation of mankind."[175]

When they are righteous, men who hold this priesthood are able to give what is called a "priesthood blessing" which is where they lay their hands on the head of someone else and act as God's mouthpiece, telling the person whatever He (i.e. God) wants them to know. As they come from God, priesthood blessings are deeply personal and can be binding as long as the person follows the instructions given since it is God's will that is represented and not the person giving the blessing.

I suspect that when Isaac called Esau to him he was not completely unaware of how his son's actions had jeopardised his ability to receive all of the blessings from God that he otherwise could have had. For all we know, when Isaac was going to eat with and bless his son he may have intended to also call him to repentance and instruct him on what he needed to do to become better. We will never know because Esau is not the one who receives this blessing.

Here is the blessing that Jacob received:

"Therefore God give thee of the dew of heaven, and the fatness of the earth, and plenty of corn and wine: Let people serve thee, and nations bow down to thee: be lord over thy brethren, and let thy mother's sons bow down to thee: cursed *be* every one that curseth thee, and blessed *be* he that blesseth thee."[176]

I don't know about you but that sounds pretty good. No wonder Isaac may have wanted to give that blessing to his favorite son. Now Esau was a skilled hunter remember so although it would take him some time to get the game he was after it wouldn't take him forever. Jacob had to get out of there fast.

"And it came to pass, as soon as Isaac had made an end of blessing Jacob, and Jacob was yet scarce gone out from the presence of Isaac his father, that Esau his brother came in from his hunting. And he also had made savoury meat, and brought it unto his father, and said unto his father, Let my father arise, and eat of his son's venison, that thy soul may bless me."[177] Uh oh. This isn't going to be good.

"And Isaac his father said unto him, Who *art* thou? And he said, I *am* thy son, thy firstborn Esau. And Isaac trembled very exceedingly, and said, Who? where *is* he that hath taken venison, and brought *it* me, and I have eaten of all before thou camest, and have blessed him? **yea, *and* he shall be blessed**." [178]

The line "yea, and he shall be blessed" is the reason that I believe that this was not just what Isaac had hoped to say but what God did as well to the right person. Isaac had no power to ensure that these blessings could be carried out after his death - only God could do that. When Esau hears that Jacob had already come in and received a blessing he is very upset.

"And when Esau heard the words of his father, he cried with a great and exceeding bitter cry, and said unto his father, **Bless me, *even* me also, O my father**."[179]

No one likes to always be second best. Despite his being favored by his father, Esau may always have envied Jacob. They were twins but they did have different strengths and weaknesses. Perhaps as he gathered his hunting equipment that day he thought "finally my time is coming". Then because he had obeyed his father and left for a little while his brother had once again gotten the upper hand. Despite his plea to Isaac, his father isn't able to go against the will of God and he knows it.

"And [Isaac] said, Thy brother came with subtilty, and hath taken away thy blessing. And [Esau] said, Is not he rightly named Jacob? for he hath supplanted me these two times: he took away my birthright; and, behold, now he hath taken away my blessing. And he said, **Hast thou not reserved a blessing for me**? And Isaac answered and said unto Esau, Behold, I have made him thy lord, and all his brethren have I given to him for servants; and with corn and wine have I sustained him: and what shall I do now unto thee, my son? And Esau said unto his father, **Hast thou but one blessing, my father? bless me,** *even* **me also, O my father**. And Esau lifted up his voice, and wept." [180]

Whether Esau just wanted his father's declaration of what Isaac wanted for his future, or if he is showing faith here by acknowledging that God has blessings for everyone, he shows his determination to succeed. He is rewarded with a blessing that may not be as good as Jacob's but does show God's love for him and that he will have a great future himself.

"And Isaac his father answered and said unto him, Behold, thy dwelling shall be the fatness of the earth, and of the dew of heaven from above; And by thy sword shalt thou live, and shalt serve thy brother; and it shall come to pass when thou shalt have the dominion, that thou shalt break his yoke from off thy neck."[181]

In a way Esau already lived by the sword through his role of being a hunter so the fact that he would continue to do so isn't overly surprising. He is also promised prosperity through the phrase "thy dwelling shall be the fatness of the earth, and of the dew of heaven from above". The most significant promise though is that he and his descendants would not always serve Jacob. Eventually they would become independent of him.

Now we are led to understand that Esau did not think these blessings were good enough because he holds a grudge against Jacob.

"And Esau hated Jacob because of the blessing wherewith his father blessed him: and Esau said in his heart, The days of mourning for my father are at hand; then will I slay my brother Jacob."[182]

Now many of us when we are upset say things that we do not mean. Although we all know that this is a form of lying since we would never be able to follow through on our threats we still do it because in a way blowing off steam like this helps us to feel better. That does not seem to be the case here. We do not know if Esau was known for being a man prone to violence or not but those who heard him say these words knew that he was serious. He was angry and bitter enough to actually take the life of his brother but considerate enough of his father to not do it while he was alive. Eventually his mother finds out what he has been saying and once again takes matters into her own hands in order to protect her son from himself.

"And these words of Esau her elder son were told to Rebekah: and she sent and called Jacob her younger son, and said unto him, Behold, thy brother Esau, as touching thee, doth comfort himself, *purposing* to kill thee. Now therefore, my son, obey my voice; and arise, flee thou to Laban my brother to Haran; And tarry with him a few days, until thy brother's fury turn away; Until thy brother's anger turn away from thee, and he forget *that* which thou hast done to him: then I will send, and fetch thee from thence: why should I be deprived also of you both in one day? And Rebekah said to Isaac, I am weary of my life because of the daughters of Heth: if Jacob take a wife of the daughters of Heth, such as these *which are* of the daughters of the land, what good shall my life do me?"[183]

We are not told who let Rebekah know what Esau was saying or if Isaac knew about it as well. My guess would be that unless Isaac was mainly a figurehead by this point and Rebekah was the one who made most of the family decisions (after all she does not appear to have as many health problems as her husband) he knew. As the leader of the clan it would be very surprising if he had not been made aware of the animosity that existed between Esau and Jacob. Even if he did not know how deeply Esau hated Jacob he **had** witnessed his son's reaction when he realised that Jacob had beaten him to his blessing. Whether Isaac agreed with his wife strictly on the grounds of ensuring that the covenant line remains pure and/or wanted to prevent his favoured son from becoming a murderer he sends Jacob off to visit Rebekah's family. This would have been a hard thing for both parents. They were no longer young and would have no way of knowing if he would return before they died.

Jacob's departure is described in Genesis 28:1-5. Witnessing it Esau appears to finally realise that some of the decisions **he** has made have resulted in where he has ended up and decides to try making a better choice in who he marries.

"When Esau saw that Isaac had blessed Jacob, and sent him away to Padan-aram, to take him a wife from thence; and that as he blessed him he gave him a charge, saying, Thou shalt not take a wife of the daughters of Canaan; And that Jacob obeyed his father and his mother, and was gone to Padan-aram; And **Esau seeing that the daughters of Canaan pleased not Isaac his father**; Then went Esau unto Ishmael, and took unto the wives which he had Mahalath the daughter of Ishmael Abraham's son, the sister of Nebajoth, to be his wife."[184]

Esau could not turn back the clock. Unless he wanted to act dishonourably by abandoning his wives and children he could not start over again and begin his married life by marrying into the covenant. Knowing this he tries to fix the situation by marrying into the family of Abraham through his great uncle Ishmael's line. It doesn't regain him the blessings of the Abrahamic covenant but at least it shows that he had become aware that he needed to do some changing.

As often happens in the scriptures there is silence about Esau for the next twenty years. The story focuses on Jacob and his family so we do not know what happened to Esau during the time Jacob was absent from the family. We do know however that he was made aware that Jacob was returning from Padam-Aram and decides to go meet him.

There are two problems with this decision:

1) The last time the two brothers saw each other Esau wanted to kill Jacob,

2) Esau had 400 men with him which made it look like he was not just going to attack them but completely destroy them. Not good.

"And Jacob lifted up his eyes, and looked, and, behold, Esau came, and with him four hundred men. And he divided the children unto Leah, and unto Rachel, and unto the two handmaids. And he put the handmaids and their children foremost, and Leah and her children after, and Rachel and Joseph hindermost. And he passed over before them, and bowed himself to the ground seven times, until he came near to his brother."[185]

I'd be afraid too in this situation but fortunately there was no attack coming. Although Jacob didn't know it. Esau was no longer angry with him and was happy to see his brother once again. "And Esau ran to meet him, and embraced him, and fell on his neck, and kissed him: and they wept."[186] To me this is one of the most touching scenes in the Bible. We have nothing in their history to show that Esau and Jacob were physically affectionate when they were younger. That Esau ran up to him and hugged him shows how much he loved and had missed his brother. Perhaps he had learned the meaning behind the phrase "absence makes the heart grow fonder" as he had gone years without seeing the man that had been a part of his life since he was born. Maybe it was the death of his mother and the approaching death of his father that had made him value his blood relatives more. We don't know the whys except that Esau had seen the Lord's blessings in his life and had come to accept that Jacob was the one who would receive the blessings of the Abrahamic covenant and not him. What an incredible moment this must have been for the two of them as they hugged, kissed, and cried together after two decades of separation. In addition to seeing his brother again, one of the greatest things Esau was able to have is a chance to meet his niece and nephews.

"And [Esau] lifted up his eyes, and saw the women and the children; and said, Who *are* those with thee? And [Jacob] said, The children which God hath graciously given thy servant. Then the handmaidens came near, they and their children, and they bowed themselves. And Leah also with her children came near, and bowed themselves: and after came Joseph near and Rachel, and they bowed themselves."[187] There was another thing on Esau's mind. Before he and his band of 400 men had come upon Jacob and his group Jacob had sent him several presents[188]. Esau wondered why.

"And [Esau] said, What *meanest* thou by all this drove which I met? And [Jacob] said, *These are* to find grace in the sight of my lord. And Esau said, **I have enough, my brother; keep that thou hast unto thyself**. And Jacob said, Nay, I pray thee, if now I have found grace in thy sight, then receive my present at my hand: for therefore I have seen thy face, as though I had seen the face of God, and thou wast pleased with me. Take, I pray thee, my blessing that is brought to thee; because God hath dealt graciously with me, and because I have enough. And he urged him, and he took *it*."[189]

Esau was content with what he had. He didn't want or need Jacob's gift but did accept it after his brother's urging. While we can't know all of his reasons I suspect that as he was able to look back over his life and see how he had been blessed. He may also have received revelation from God during those years and may have spent more time with his father, learning about his faith and the experiences Isaac himself had had with God.

After talking for a while Esau encouraged his brother to travel with him near where he lived but Jacob had other ideas. "And [Esau] said, Let us take our journey, and let us go, and I will go before thee. And [Jacob] said unto him, My lord knoweth that the children *are* tender, and the flocks and herds with young *are* with me: and if men should overdrive them one day, all the flock will die. Let my lord, I pray thee, pass over before his servant: and I will lead on softly, according as the cattle that goeth before me and the children be able to endure, until I come unto my lord unto Seir. And Esau said, Let me now leave with thee *some* of the folk that *are* with me. And he said, What needeth it? let me find grace in the sight of my lord. So Esau returned that day on his way unto Seir."[190]

Once again the text is irritatingly silent on whether the brothers saw each other again before the death of their father. We do know though that they together buried their father. "And Jacob came unto Isaac his father unto Mamre, unto the city of Arbah, which *is* Hebron, where Abraham and Isaac sojourned. And the days of Isaac were an hundred and fourscore years. And Isaac gave up the ghost, and died, and was gathered unto his people, *being* old and full of days: and his sons Esau and Jacob buried him."[191]

So, what happened to Esau after his father's death? I'm not sure. What we do know is that like his brother he had many sons and as a result was the patriarch of many different nations. [192] He was also very wealthy. So wealthy in fact that like Lot and Abraham[193] before him he and his brother had to part ways because, like in an old western, "the land just wasn't big enough for the two of them".

"And Esau took his wives, and his sons, and his daughters, and all the persons of his house, and his cattle, and all his beasts, and all his substance, which he had got in the land of Canaan; and went into the country from the face of his brother Jacob. For their riches were more than that they might dwell together; and the land wherein they were strangers could not bear them because of their cattle."[194]

Where and when he died is not given but his descendents became very powerful in their own right fulfilling the promises of the Lord to him in that blessing so many years before.

So, what can Esau teach us?

1. Your past mistakes do not mean it is game over.

Esau lost out on some of the spiritual blessings he as the first born may have had because of his choice to marry outside the covenant. Even though he did try to repent by marrying into the Ishmaelite nation later on he could not regain those blessings after they were gone. Nevertheless, he still ended his life well - he had many children, many servants and fighting men, and was very wealthy according to the standards of that time. At the end of his life he is content with what he has and appears to be more grateful for his remaining family members. His father Isaac appears to continue to be proud of him when he dies and he and his brother have reconciled. While he never verbally praises the Lord he may also have developed his faith as he grew older and may have done great things since his death.

2. God does not just have blessings reserved for some of his children.

I do not agree with the direction that Rebekah chose to take when dealing with her sons. I will not judge her however because I do not know what was going on in her head. I do believe however that the end result of that story of deception and betrayal was what God had intended to occur. As mentioned earlier I believe that the blessings given to both Jacob and Esau were Priesthood Blessings and not from Isaac their father. If I am right then Esau was not cheated out of the blessings that God intended for him. Although he hadn't been completely obedient, and had thus forfeited some of the blessings he could have had, he did not have a rebellious heart either and had been obedient to other commandments and was thus entitled to those blessings. Unlike Cain, Esau respected his father and mother and when he finally realised that he had disappointed them he tried to make things right. As a result, he did end up with the things he had been promised in his blessing - wealth, numerous posterity, and independence from his brother.

3. You are the writer of your own future.

After Jacob was gone Esau could no longer blame him for the things that went wrong in his life nor could he receive his brother's help in achieving the blessings he had been promised. Also, while he could go to his parents and in-laws for advice there was little that they could do for him. He was the one who was responsible for making sure those blessings happened. It is a shame that we do not have more of his story in the Bible because it would be interesting to see how this man was able to achieve the things that he did in the 20 years before his story starts up again. By following his example many people could also gain greatness and receive the blessings from the Lord that they are due.

Shechem - Prince with a Problem.

I think that as a woman this is one of the hardest people in the scriptures to write about but out of my commitment to be fair in this book I think that we do need to give Shechem his due. Shechem is one of the many people in the scriptures whose motives are the most ambiguous. Very little is written about him and what we do have could be taken many different ways.

Shechem's brief story comes to us in Genesis 34 and right off the bat he doesn't endear himself to us at all.

"And Dinah the daughter of Leah, which she bare unto Jacob, went out to see the daughters of the land. And when Shechem the son of Hamor the Hivite, prince of the country, saw her, he took her, and lay with her, and defiled her."[195]

Dinah, the only known daughter of Jacob, was the last of Jacob's children with his wife Leah making her number 11 out of Jacob's 13 children[196]. We do not know the details her childhood, other than knowing the events that she would have lived through from the stories of her parents, however we can assume that since all of her full brothers and most of her half brothers were older than her she was probably well looked after and protected. According to these verses one day she went to

131

visit some friends when Shechem saw her. We do not know if she was alone or had a chaperone with her, which Shechem would have had to get rid of in order to take Dinah away, but it doesn't matter. Either scenario would have made this a very scary situation for her. The text doesn't say whether this was their first meeting or if they had an existing relationship, even on the acquaintance level. I hope it is the former because otherwise what happened would have been even more of a betrayal for her. To defile someone is to violate their chastity. [197] This combined with the phrase "he took her" indicates that Dinah was not given a choice by Shechem: he forced her to have sex with him. Not only would being raped have been traumatic for her just by itself but, as the daughter of a prophet, she would have known that the Lord values chastity highly and may, like many rape victims, have blamed herself for what happened. The truth is we don't know what she was thinking or how traumatic the situation was for her but we can assume from the text that Shechem felt bad about what had happened and wanted to make it right.

"And his soul clave unto Dinah the daughter of Jacob, and he loved the damsel, and spake kindly unto the damsel."[198]

We have no idea how long Shechem had Dinah in his household, how/why he felt so close to her, how she felt about him in return, or what the "kind words" he said to her were. Thankfully, as the word kindly is used to describe the conversation, he probably did not make her feel like she was to blame. He now had a big decision to make: either cast her aside and not take responsibility for his actions, like David's son Amnon did when he raped his half-sister Tamar[199], or he could do the honourable thing and marry her. He chose the latter.

"And Shechem spake unto his father Hamor, saying, Get me this damsel to wife. And Jacob heard that he had defiled Dinah his daughter: now his sons were with his cattle in the field: and Jacob held his peace until they were come. And Hamor the father of Shechem went out unto Jacob to commune with him."[200]

Shechem's conversation with his father, and his subsequent actions, show us though that his marriage proposal was sincere and not just an attempt to look like he was doing the right thing. As a North American the fact that he sends his father over to talk to her father sounds cowardly until I recall a conversation I had with a co-worker while I was in university. I once worked with a gentleman from Pakistan who had an arranged marriage and was waiting for his fiancée to come join him here in Canada. In response to my questions about it he explained that in his culture the parents are the ones who arrange weddings. He went on to explain that if a young man wants to marry a particular young woman, he sends his parents over to her house to make the request of her parents on his behalf. The parents do the negotiation and the young woman is given the option of accepting the marriage proposal or politely declining. The families will then arrange a get together where, after having an opportunity to watch how they each interact with their existing family members and each other's family, the children still have one more chance to say yes or no to the marriage before the engagement is official. A similar scenario was demonstrated in the movie "The Kite Runner". Assuming that marriages were arranged similarly in their culture, Shechem appears to be doing the honourable thing by offering to marry Dinah and was willing to show it by following the protocol of the day.

"And the sons of Jacob came out of the field when they heard *it:* and the men were grieved, and they were very wroth, because he had wrought folly in Israel in lying with Jacob's daughter; **which thing ought not to be done**. And Hamor communed with them, saying, The soul of my son Shechem longeth for your daughter: I pray you give her him to wife. And make ye marriages with us, *and* give your daughters unto us, and take our daughters unto you. And ye shall dwell with us: and the land shall be before you; dwell and trade ye therein, and get you possessions therein. And Shechem said unto her father and unto her brethren, Let me find grace in your eyes, and what ye shall say unto me I will give. Ask me never so much dowry and gift, and I will give according as ye shall say unto me: but give me the damsel to wife."[201]

I really feel for Hamor in this scenario. We don't know what he was like as a person or many other details about him that would help us know how he felt about the situation:

- How did Hamor feel about Dinah - did he even want her as a daughter-in-law?
- Did Hamor know Dinah before her rape? If so, then this would have been something that would have been personal.
- What was his relationship with Shechem like - were they close or distant?

- Was this the first time Shechem had done anything like this or was he known for taking what he wanted regardless of the consequences? If it was the latter then this may not have been the first time Hamor had had to clean up his son's mess.
- What were his plans regarding his son? Most parents have dreams for their children. As a king, he probably did as well.

Hopefully he disapproved of Shechem's actions and had rebuked his son for raping a girl once he found out. Maybe Shechem was betrothed to another and this would jeopardise that alliance. Regardless of Hamor's personal feelings, as Shechem's father, he was the "lucky" person who had to go and face Dinah's family. As a parent, who may have had daughters of his own, he had to know that it wasn't going to go well - no father wants to hear that a crime has been committed against his child and her family had a right to be angry. Hopefully, as he went to talk to them he was also looking out for Dinah and wanted to assist in helping take away her disgrace by marrying her to the man she had slept with - albeit against her will. His response shows that he definitely wanted to strengthen relations between the two nations through future marriages. Whether this strengthening was intended to be strictly political or because he wanted to have family bonds is unclear.

Fortunately for Hamor he didn't go alone to this meeting. Shechem also went to face the music. Shechem offers to give them **anything** they want in order to marry Dinah. Now granted as a prince he was probably very wealthy but even so I doubt that it would have been the normal thing to do. The amount of a dowry was probably set or at least had guidelines so that the families would be able to come to an agreement that was suitable for both of them. Instead, I'm inclined to believe that he couldn't come up with a suitable price on his own in order to show his sincerity and instead was willing to pay whatever they said either out of love for her or out of punishment for his crime. Unfortunately for both Shechem and Hamor, what they didn't count on was just how angry Dinah's brothers were and how they would seek their revenge. First they lied to and tricked them and, by default, made them lie to their people. Then they not only killed **Shechem**, the person that they actually had a reason to be angry at, but **all** of the men in his city. Not fair or right Simeon and Levi.

"And the sons of Jacob answered Shechem and Hamor his father **deceitfully**, and said, because he had defiled Dinah their sister: ... We cannot do this thing, to give our sister to one that is uncircumcised; for that *were* a reproach unto us: But in this will we consent unto you: If ye will be as we *be,* that every male of you be circumcised; Then will we give our daughters unto you, and we will take your daughters to us, and we will dwell with you, and we will become one people. But if ye will not hearken unto us, to be circumcised; then will we take our daughter, and we will be gone. And their words pleased Hamor, and Shechem Hamor's son. **And the young man deferred not to do the thing**, because he had delight in Jacob's daughter: and **he *was* more honourable than all the house of his father**. And Hamor and Shechem his son came unto the gate of their city, and communed with the men of their city, saying, These men *are* peaceable with us; therefore let them dwell in the land, and trade therein; for the land, behold, *it is* large enough for them; let us take their daughters to us for wives, and let us give them our daughters. Only herein will the men consent unto us for to dwell with us, to be one people, if every male among us be circumcised, as they *are* circumcised. *Shall* not their cattle and their substance and every beast of theirs *be* ours? only let us consent unto them, and they will dwell with us. And unto Hamor and unto Shechem his son hearkened all that went out of the gate of his city; and every male was circumcised, all that went out of the gate of his city. And it came to pass on the third day, when they were sore, that two of the sons of Jacob, Simeon and Levi, Dinah's brethren, took each man his sword, and came upon the city boldly, and slew all the males. And they slew Hamor and Shechem his son with the edge of the sword, and took Dinah out of Shechem's house, and went out. The sons of Jacob came upon the slain, and spoiled the city, because they had defiled their sister. They took their sheep, and their oxen, and their asses, and that which *was* in the city, and that which *was* in the field, And all their wealth, and all their little ones, and their wives took they captive, and spoiled even all that *was* in the house."[202]

The tragedy factor of this story is high due to the size of the victim count involved.

First there is Dinah who was raped, detained against her will, and almost forced into marriage to her rapist.

Then there are the people of the city who, after obeying the command of their king and prince to make peace with their neighbours, are killed, robbed, and/or have their families destroyed by Jacob's sons. Hamor is also a victim in that he was killed as a result of **his son's** actions and not his own.

Lastly, although he is also the perpetrator of a crime, Shechem is a victim in that he is killed out of revenge despite trying to make amends. There is absolutely no excuse for what Shechem did - rape is ALWAYS a crime. No one should ever be forced to do something against their will and what he did to Dinah was horrible but I feel we really shouldn't judge him unfairly. From the text he is described as being "more honourable than all the house of his father"[203] indicating that he was "deserving of honour, of great renown, accompanied with marks of honor, and/or characterized by integrity"[204]. If all of these definitions apply to him then Shechem was in general a good man, liked and respected by those who knew him, who made a horrible mistake and was killed before he fully had a chance to repent. Only God and he truly know why he went down the road that he did. He may have wanted to marry Dinah for political reasons, after all he does talk about the wealth Jacob had when trying to convince his men to be circumcised, however we cannot know if that was all - he may really have fallen in love with her. Maybe his motivation is that he had loved her for a while and wanted to force her father's hand since he knew Jacob wouldn't consent otherwise. The fact that he was willing to go through a very painful procedure to be able to marry Dinah shows that he was serious - cowards or someone who was not serious would probably have backed down or tried to get out of it instead of going through the pain. We'll never know. As for me I hope that he has repented and that she was able to find happiness despite what happened to her.

What can Shechem's story teach us:

1) **We don't live in a consequence bubble.**

Shechem's actions did not just affect him. His father, mother (if she was alive), siblings (if applicable), people, the woman he loved, and her family were all affected in significant ways by these events. Many people lost their lives, Dinah lost her innocence and possibly her love (if she had fallen for him as well), and Simeon and Levi became murderers. None of it was necessary or what God has ever wanted for His children yet the consequences of his actions snowballed into something larger than he may have anticipated or was able to stop.

2) **Fairness should be applied on both sides in a crime.**

One of Shechem's biggest failures in this story is that he did not fulfill his responsibility as a man to protect women and instead harmed one. No amount of apologising would ever take that away from them. I think that he regretted it and hope that he **tried** at least to understand how much he had hurt her even if he never quite managed it. One thing I can say for certainty - if he didn't regret it then he probably does now and would not want us to follow his example.

Then there is Dinah. Years ago a young man who I thought I knew well enough to trust betrayed me by losing his temper one night and pulling a gun on someone close to me. I was not there but heard about it before the night was over and it had a significant effect on me. In one instant my world came crashing down around me. For a long time afterwards I had trouble trusting new people because my mind kept telling me "you can't trust your instincts. You were wrong about him and you could be wrong about someone else." The reason I bring this up is because I hope that Dinah was eventually able to leave the trauma of the past behind her and didn't let what happened affect her relationship with men, including her future husband if she did marry someone else. That would not have been fair to him or to her. As a victim she was not guilty and deserved to have a happy life. Let's hope that she did.

Now on to the brothers. As a rule I do not believe in capital punishment for every crime although I do think that there are scenarios where it is justified to protect the future victims of a person who has **proven that they will keep committing the same crime**. A person who refuses to stop hurting others should be prevented from doing so permanently if necessary. I also disagree with the tendency some people have to blame **every** member of a community, nation, or ethnic group for the actions of **only one or a few of its members.** I've seen that tendency in my own life following the events of September 11, 2001 and along with other North Americans can look back with regret on the internment camps that were set up during World War 2.

Levi and Simeon were not justified in what they did. The rape of their sister by Shechem may have justified them to take their revenge out on him, I'm not going to play judge or jury on that, but they had **no right** to lie to him or to take it out on the people in his town. That was wrong. True, it can be argued that by not stopping their prince his people were guilty as well by omission if not commission but can we really be sure of that? How aware were the German people of everything the Nazis were doing during World War 2? All it says is that

Shechem took her. Where he raped her is not indicated and his people may not have known that she was a victim who was being held against her will. Another thing to consider is that Shechem may have apologised and it just wasn't recorded. We don't know. If he did, they should have tried to determine his sincerity before continuing on with their decision.

Had Simeon and Levi been honest and said "no you can't have her because of what you did to her", instead of tricking him in order to make him vulnerable, they could have remained victims in this scenario. Instead, they lied and killed becoming just as guilty, in a different way, as the one who had hurt their sister. Did they even think about that? Did they even spare a thought towards the families that they would be harming as theirs had been? I suspect not or else they may not have gone through with it. May we not follow their example and let our emotions control us and cause us to do wrong.

Pharoah - Prophetic Dreamer and Famine Thwarter

One of the best-known stories of the Bible is that of how Joseph, after being sold as a slave and put in prison for a crime he didn't commit, interpreted Pharaoh's dreams, became his second in command, and saved the Israelites and other nations from starvation. While I am a fan of Joseph's, and consider him to be a man that we should aspire to become like, he has been admired for thousands of years and thus has had his time in the sun. Let's look at the other man of significance in this story. By this I mean the Pharaoh. He was the one who received the dreams remember and that says something about how God felt about him.

OK so like Abimelech who we met in a previous chapter we are introduced to the leader of a country who is not a member of the house of Israel yet he is the one whom God chooses to warn about an upcoming famine. Famines are not new to us - both Abraham and Isaac ended up moving because of famines in previous chapters of Genesis yet we have nothing recorded in the text to indicate that they, or anyone else, was warned in advance that the famine was coming. Egypt appears in these stories to have fared well during these times of hunger, probably because it was on the Nile. For reasons known only to God this time He decides to shake things up a bit and let one of the leaders of a nation, instead of His prophet Jacob who you would expect Him to talk to, know that there will be a famine in the future.

Our story with this Pharaoh begins after Joseph has been in prison two years following his interpretation of the dreams of the baker and chief butler of the Pharaoh in Genesis 40. It was a dark and restless night.

"And it came to pass at the end of two full years, that Pharaoh dreamed: and, behold, he stood by the river. And, behold, there came up out of the river seven well favoured kine and fat fleshed; and they fed in a meadow. And, behold, seven other kine came up after them out of the river, ill favoured and lean fleshed; and stood by the *other* kine upon the brink of the river. And the ill favoured and lean fleshed kine did eat up the seven well favoured and fat kine. **So Pharaoh awoke**. And he slept and dreamed the second time: and, behold, seven ears of corn came up upon one stalk, rank and good. And, behold, seven thin ears and blasted with the east wind sprung up after them. And the seven thin ears devoured the seven rank and full ears. **And Pharaoh awoke, and, behold, *it was* a dream**."[205]

Now to me living in modern day Canada and having seen more than one horror movie in my life dreaming about cattle that eat each other and ears of grain that do the same would probably not scare me enough to wake me up not once but twice. I do not know how much warfare this Pharaoh may have seen or if he was a man that scared easily. I also don't know if Pharaoh was a dreamer or not. I very rarely remember or am aware of my dreams. Other people I've met dream nightly. Pharaoh could have been anywhere along this scale. Even if Pharoah dreamed regularly, these were no ordinary dreams for him. He recognised right away that they were significant and was paying close attention because he is able to describe them in detail to other people.

"And it came to pass in the morning that his spirit was troubled; and he sent and called for all the magicians of Egypt, and all the wise men thereof: and Pharaoh told them his dream; but *there was* none that could interpret them unto Pharaoh."[206]

We can assume from his future actions that this Pharaoh was an intelligent man. We can also assume that because he was royalty that he was probably well educated. He had many advisors, and he listened to them, so he understood the lesson taught by King Solomon centuries later that "[w]ithout counsel purposes are disappointed: but in the multitude of counsellors they are established."[207] His advisors would also have been wise and intelligent. Now considering that I find it hard to believe that they told him nothing. Chances are good that they did give him an interpretation for his dreams but none of their ideas felt quite right to him so he knew that they hadn't been interpreted properly.

All around him knew how important this was to him and finally one of his loyal servants spoke up.

"Then spake the chief butler unto Pharaoh, saying, I do remember my faults this day: Pharaoh was wroth with his servants, and put me in ward in the captain of the guard's house, *both* me and the chief baker: And we dreamed a dream in one night, I and he; we dreamed each man according to the interpretation of his dream. And *there was* there with us a young man, an Hebrew, servant to the captain of the guard; and we told him, and he interpreted to us our dreams; to each man according to his dream he did interpret. And it came to pass, as he interpreted to us, so it was; me he restored unto mine office, and him he hanged."[208]

Now the testimony of this servant must have been very powerful because Pharaoh acts immediately.

"Then Pharaoh sent and called Joseph, and they brought him hastily out of the dungeon: and he shaved *himself,* and changed his raiment, and came in unto Pharaoh."[209]

We have no way of knowing if he recognised Joseph. If Pharaoh had ever visited Potiphar's house while Joseph was his slave it is possible that he had seen Joseph before. Regardless Pharaoh was a man of power and he expected people to reverence him. We don't know if he asked Joseph any questions before the recorded beginning of their conversation but from what we do have Pharaoh goes first.

"And Pharaoh said unto Joseph, I have dreamed a dream, and *there is* none that can interpret it: and I have heard say of thee, *that* thou canst understand a dream to interpret it."[210]

In a way this is a test because by observing how Joseph reacts to him and his command this Pharaoh can gauge a bit about his character. While Pharaoh was desperate to get an answer he really had nothing to lose in this situation. There are wise men and magicians in every court so even if his can't give him an answer surely one from an allies' court could help out this Pharaoh. If Joseph fails then he'll end up back in prison or in the executioners' hands while Pharaoh will continue searching for his answer until he finds it. How will the young man react? Surprisingly, despite his low status and unexpected, spontaneous release from prison Joseph responds to Pharaoh with confidence, intelligence, and respect not fear or confusion.

"And Joseph answered Pharaoh, saying, *It is* **not in me: God shall give Pharaoh an answer of peace**."[211]

Whether this impressed Pharaoh or not it did give him the incentive to give this stranger a chance. Once again Pharaoh describes his dream to another person hoping that they can help him to understand it's meaning.

"And Pharaoh said unto Joseph, In my dream, behold, I stood upon the bank of the river: And, behold, there came up out of the river seven kine, fat fleshed and well favoured; and they fed in a meadow: And, behold, seven other kine came up after them, poor and very ill favoured and lean fleshed, such as I never saw in all the land of Egypt for badness: And the lean and the ill favoured kine did eat up the first seven fat kine: And when they had eaten them up, it could not be known that they had eaten them; but they *were* still ill favoured, as at the beginning. So I awoke. And I saw in my dream, and, behold, seven ears came up in one stalk, full and good: And, behold, seven ears, withered, thin, *and* blasted with the east wind, sprung up after them: And the thin ears devoured the seven good ears: and **I told *this* unto the magicians; but *there***
***was* none that could declare *it* to me**."[212]

In Pharaoh's final declaration he once again tells Joseph the reason he has been released from prison - no one else had been able to tell Pharaoh what his dream meant. Depending on the tone that he told his story in Joseph may also have been able to tell how much the answer really meant to him. While he may have intended to reward Joseph if he was able to give him an answer Pharaoh probably didn't realise what the ultimate result of their conversation would be.

"And Joseph said unto Pharaoh, The dream of Pharaoh *is* one: **God hath shewed Pharaoh what he *is* about to do**. The seven good kine *are* seven years; and the seven good ears *are* seven years: the dream *is* one. And the seven thin and ill favoured kine that came up after them *are* seven years; and the seven empty ears blasted with the east wind shall be seven years of famine. This *is* the thing which I have spoken unto Pharaoh: **What God *is* about to do he sheweth unto Pharaoh**. Behold, there come seven years of great plenty throughout all the land of Egypt: And there shall arise after them seven years of famine; and all the plenty shall be forgotten in the land of Egypt; and the famine shall consume the land; And the plenty shall not be known in the land by reason of that famine following; for it *shall be* very grievous. And for that the dream was doubled unto Pharaoh twice; ***it is* because the thing *is* established by God, and God will shortly bring it to pass**." [213]

Now we know from their tombs and other surviving records that the ancient Egyptians were very religious people. Assuming that this Pharaoh was as well Joseph's initial answer, which reiterated three times that the dream he received was from God, would probably have made him sit up and pay attention because it reinforced what he had already believed - this was an important dream that he needed an answer to. The answer was terrifying - a famine was coming that was going to be like NOTHING they had ever seen before. Now as the leader of his nation Pharaoh would have had to come up with a plan of how they were going to handle this. And then this young, former slave/prisoner may have surprised him by giving him the answer without being asked for it first.

"Now therefore let Pharaoh look out a man discreet and wise, and set him over the land of Egypt. Let Pharaoh do *this,* and let him appoint officers over the land, and take up the fifth part of the land of Egypt in the seven plenteous years. And let them gather all the food of those good years that come, and lay up corn under the hand of Pharaoh, and let them keep food in the cities. And that food shall be for store to the land against the seven years of famine, which shall be in the land of Egypt; that the land perish not through the famine."[214]

This suggested plan is impressive for a couple of reasons.

- First, it shows Joseph's experience with administration and delegation. Joseph knew that this was going to take a team of people to pull off with one person in charge to supervise, motivate and reorganise that team as needed.
- Second, it was a feasible plan that they would be able to implement over the seven years they had to prepare. Joseph wasn't suggesting that they wait and then scramble at the last minute. By doing this gradually over time Pharaoh's people would be unhappy that they would have to give up a portion of

their crops but would be less likely to panic when the disaster came.

- Third, it was a no-lose situation. If Joseph was wrong then Pharaoh would have a bunch of grain stored but he could always gradually sell or trade it at a profit or use it for another purpose. If Joseph was right in his interpretation, then they would fare far better during the seven-year famine than their neighbours who would have only the remains of their last season's crops. No wonder Pharaoh was impressed.

"And the thing was good in the eyes of Pharaoh, and in the eyes of all his servants. And Pharaoh said unto his servants, Can we find *such a one* as this *is,* **a man in whom the Spirit of God** *is?*"[215]

Now here is where we get to see the great leader that this Pharaoh was. He liked the plan because he realised that not only was it logical but also realised that it came from God so did not question it at all. He also must have been thoroughly impressed by Joseph. I do not believe for one second that Pharaoh did not have men in his household or court already who could have carried out the plan. Although his advisors and magicians had failed in their interpretation of his dreams he must have had military leaders, courtiers, or other people of high rank that would have had the skills necessary to pull off this plan. Pharaoh had no reason to go with an unknown Hebrew who may have proven himself in supervisory roles in the past but had recently gotten out of prison no matter how charismatic that man may be. Yet he did and I suspect it was because Joseph was a man "in whom the Spirit of God is." Pharaoh realised that if Joseph held himself accountable to God first then he would not try to cheat Pharaoh or his people.

"And Pharaoh said unto Joseph, Forasmuch as God hath shewed thee all this, *there is* none so discreet and wise as thou *art:* Thou shalt be over my house, and according unto thy word shall all my people be ruled: only in the throne will I be greater than thou. And Pharaoh said unto Joseph, See, I have set thee over all the land of Egypt. And Pharaoh took off his ring from his hand, and put it upon Joseph's hand, and arrayed him in vestures of fine linen, and put a gold chain about his neck; And he made him to ride in the second chariot which he had; and they cried before him, Bow the knee: and he made him *ruler* over all the land of Egypt. And Pharaoh said unto Joseph, I *am* Pharaoh, and without thee shall no man lift up his hand or foot in all the land of Egypt. And Pharaoh called Joseph's name Zaphnath-paaneah; and he gave him to wife Asenath the daughter of Poti-pherah priest of On. And Joseph went out over *all* the land of Egypt."[216]

Pharaoh needed to make Joseph as acceptable to the Egyptians as he could. New name, Egyptian wife from the priestly lineage, status symbols, and Pharaoh's personal endorsement. Not bad. He was taking a big risk but Joseph did not let him down.

"And Joseph *was* thirty years old when he stood before Pharaoh king of Egypt. And Joseph went out from the presence of Pharaoh, and went throughout all the land of Egypt. And in the seven plenteous years the earth brought forth by handfuls. And he gathered up all the food of the seven years, which were in the land of Egypt, and laid up the food in the cities: the food of the field, which *was* round about every city, laid he up in the same. And Joseph gathered corn as the sand of the sea, very much, until he left numbering; for *it was* without number.... And the seven years of plenteousness, that was in the land of Egypt, were ended. And the seven years of dearth began to come, according as Joseph had said: and the dearth was in all lands; but in all the land of Egypt there was bread. And when all the land of Egypt was famished, the people cried to Pharaoh for bread: and Pharaoh said unto all the Egyptians, Go unto Joseph; what he saith to you, do. And the famine was over all the face of the earth: And Joseph opened all the storehouses, and sold unto the Egyptians; and the famine waxed sore in the land of Egypt. And all countries came into Egypt to Joseph for to buy *corn;* because that the famine was *so* sore in all lands." [217]

Now to give you a brief synopsis of the next chapter in Joseph's story (please see Genesis 42-46 for details). The famine reaches Canaan and Joseph's ten brothers come to buy grain. They do not recognise him so he decides to test them in several different ways. After they pass his tests and he sees that they have changed he reveals who he is, lets them know that he forgives them, tells them that the famine is not over, and invites them to go get Jacob and the rest of their families so that they can all ride out the famine together in Egypt. The brothers agree and seventy people descend on Egypt. Now Joseph has to explain a few things to Pharaoh.

"Then Joseph came and told Pharaoh, and said, My father and my brethren, and their flocks, and their herds, and all that they have, are come out of the land of Canaan; and, behold, they *are* in the land of Goshen. And he took some of his brethren, *even* five men, and presented them unto Pharaoh." [218] Pharaoh trusted Joseph and we can tell that he had come to respect him so he was fine with his family coming to stay. He did have some questions for them though. "And Pharaoh said unto his brethren, What *is* your occupation? And they said unto Pharaoh, Thy servants *are* shepherds, both we, *and* also our fathers. They said moreover unto Pharaoh, For to sojourn in the land are we come; for thy servants have no pasture for their flocks; for the famine *is* sore in the land of Canaan: now therefore, we pray thee, let thy servants dwell in the land of Goshen."[219] This answer must have impressed Pharaoh because he "spake unto Joseph, saying, Thy father and thy brethren are come unto thee: The land of Egypt *is* before thee; in the best of the land make thy father and brethren to dwell; in the land of Goshen let them dwell: and if thou knowest *any* men of activity among them, then make them rulers over my cattle."[220]

To be the keeper of Pharaoh's cattle would have been a great honour for them although the text doesn't say if any of them took him up on his offer. The last person that Pharaoh was able to meet was the third major patriarch of the family - Jacob. As Joseph's father Pharaoh was probably very interested in meeting him to see if he like his son was a man of God.

"And Joseph brought in Jacob his father, and set him before Pharaoh: and **Jacob blessed Pharaoh**. And Pharaoh said unto Jacob, How old *art* thou? And Jacob said unto Pharaoh, The days of the years of my pilgrimage *are* an hundred and thirty years: few and evil have the days of the years of my life been, and have not attained unto the days of the years of the life of my fathers in the days of their pilgrimage. **And Jacob blessed Pharaoh**, and went out from before Pharaoh."[221]

Jacob was a prophet so once again it may be assumed that this was a Priesthood Blessing but we cannot be sure since the content is not recorded. Either way Pharaoh had been honoured to meet this prophet of God before his death, had saved his people from calamity, and had made a new friend in Joseph because he had followed the instructions of God in a dream many years before. What a great man.

So what can we learn from this Pharaoh?

---

1. Keep searching for answers even if you have to go to unexpected places.

Pharaoh could have given up on interpreting his dreams following the failure of his wise men and magicians. Had he done so his people would have thought they were extremely blessed during the years of plenty and then many of them would have died unnecessarily during the famine. Instead of giving up he continued to look for answers and eventually found them putting himself in a position where he could take action. That he had to go to a former slave turned prisoner for those answers was probably a very big surprise for him but nevertheless his continued searching lead to our ability to admire him instead of lamenting him for being a poor ruler.

---

2. Proper delegation of important tasks is key.

For all we know this Pharaoh could have had the intelligence and skills needed to head up the project himself but for reasons known only to him he decided not to do so. Maybe he realised he didn't have the skills required. Maybe he had other important projects on the go and wanted to focus more on them. Maybe he just felt that as a king it was beneath him to take an active role like that. What we can infer is that he wanted this project to succeed and was careful in who he set in charge of it. He had the skills and knowledge necessary to not only recognise Joseph's plan as the best one but to also realise during their short meeting that Joseph would be perfect in carrying it out.

3. Dreams do come true.

The two main men in this story - Pharaoh and Joseph - were both dreamers who had their dreams come true. In one case the dream was wonderful while the other was a nightmare. In both cases the predicted future did in fact occur. Neither one knew exactly what their dreams meant when they had them and needed someone else to understand them. Together they were able to make their dreams come true/overcome them.

Shiphrah and Puah - Israelite Midwives Extraordinaire

One of the greatest injustices in my memory is that I have never heard anyone in all of the years I have gone to church mention these two women in a significant enough way that I knew who they were before finding them while reading the Bible. Shame on us because although their story is brief and lacks detail what we do have shows us that these two women are as great examples of courage and faith as any of the well-known Bible heroes and heroines and they deserve to have their turn to be in the spotlight. Another reason we should become familiar with them is that their influence may have affected one of the greatest leaders in Israel's history - Moses.

To tell their story properly lets first set the scene. At the beginning of the book of Exodus we are told that "... Joseph died, and all his brethren, and all that generation. And the children of Israel were fruitful, and increased abundantly, and multiplied, and waxed exceeding mighty; and the land was filled with them. Now there arose up a new king over Egypt, which knew not Joseph."[222] As you know from the previous chapter, the Israelites were guests in Egypt having come there to escape a severe famine several years earlier.[223] At first they were welcome guests of the Egyptian Pharaoh because they were the family of Joseph, the man who had interpreted his dreams and saved his nation from starvation.[224] Once that Pharaoh and those who had known Joseph were gone however it appears that the Egyptian's gratitude diminished and fear and mistrust took its place.

"And [Pharoah] said unto his people, Behold, the people of the children of Israel *are* more and mightier than we: Come on, let us deal wisely with them; lest they multiply, and it come to pass, that, when there falleth out any war, they join also unto our enemies, and fight against us, and *so* get them up out of the land. Therefore they did set over them taskmasters to afflict them with their burdens. And they built for Pharaoh treasure cities, Pithom and Raamses. But the more they afflicted them, the more they multiplied and grew. And they were grieved because of the children of Israel. And the Egyptians made the children of Israel to serve with rigour: And they made their lives bitter with hard bondage, in mortar, and in brick, and in all manner of service in the field: all their service, wherein they made them serve, *was* with rigour."[225]

Now to be fair to the Egyptians the fears expressed in these verses were probably very real to them. The Israelites were outsiders who had kept themselves separate from the Egyptians. As they were not Egyptians there was no reason for the expectation of pre-existing patriotism or loyalty so their fear that Israelites would conspire against them instead of stand by them should their enemies attack was a real possibility. They may also have feared becoming the minority in their own country and losing their culture as the Israelite numbers grew - a fear still shared by many today as more and more immigrants come into their country. Ironically this was one fear that we know now was completely wrong as the Egyptian culture thrived for thousands of years after this story took place and is admired and studied to this day. Plus we know that the Egyptians probably hated the Israelites because some of their gods were cattle and the Israelites were shepherds.[226] Given these things it's not surprising the way they acted. Does it make it right to enslave your former guests - no - but that's what they did. Unfortunately for the Egyptians this plan didn't work and the Israelites thrived despite their hardships.

Okay time for Plan B.

"And the king of Egypt spake to the Hebrew midwives, of which the name of the one *was* Shiphrah, and the name of the other Puah: And he said, When ye do the office of a midwife to the Hebrew women, and see *them* upon the stools; if it *be* a son, then ye shall kill him: but if it *be* a daughter, then she shall live."[227]

Okay so let's recap the situation that Shiphrah and Puah found themselves in. They are midwives whose primary purpose is to help women during one of the most dangerous times in their lives - giving birth. They work to ensure that both mother and child make it through this event alive and well. This is an important job because then and now not all women can and do survive it. Now the most powerful man in the country has come to them and told them to do something that was against both their professional and moral ethics - kill babies. If they refuse outright he will be angry and will most likely punish them, maybe even kill them. If they go along with it they will be doing something that they know is wrong. Oh for the good old days before we came into bondage by the Egyptians.

So what did they do? They didn't go along with Pharaoh's plan because they knew that it wasn't what God wanted them to do.

"But the midwives **feared God**, and did not as the king of Egypt commanded them, but saved the men children alive." [228]

Pharaoh finds out that Plan B isn't working either and wants to know why they disobeyed him.

"And the king of Egypt called for the midwives, and said unto them, Why have ye done this thing, and have saved the men children alive? And the midwives said unto Pharaoh, Because the Hebrew women *are* not as the Egyptian women; for they *are* lively, and are delivered ere the midwives come in unto them."[229]

Okay so they lied to the Pharaoh but:

- For all we know it was partially true that not all births were attended to by the midwives so they could not have done as he asked even if they had wanted to;

- To quote Jack Nicholson in the movie <u>A Few Good Men</u> Pharaoh probably couldn't "handle the truth". What I mean is that Pharaoh either did not understand the laws of God or he didn't respect them so taking the opportunity to tell him about their trust in God may not have gone very well; and

- Their telling him the real reason would have potentially put their own lives in danger and prevented them from continuing to thwart him. They were human after all and self-preservation is a very strong motivation.

Personally, I admire them. It was not a good situation that they found themselves in and most likely not an easy decision to make. They show true courage and faith by standing by their principles during this dark time in both Egypt's and Israel's history. They didn't let their fear of Pharaoh overrule their respect and love for God and they were rewarded for it.

"Therefore God dealt well with the midwives: and the people multiplied, and waxed very mighty. And it came to pass, because the midwives feared God, that he made them houses." [230]

No God didn't build them physical houses. Like many people before them their obedience allowed God to ensure that their lines would continue for a very long time. Sadly, this is all we know about them. Their story may be short and sweet but it is no less powerful.

So what can we learn from these two great women?

1) You may be asked to do things that are against your moral and professional ethics.

Sadly, while most people are not asked to commit the murder of infants, this story is not a one-of-a-kind event. There are many stories out their where people are asked to lie, cheat, cut corners, let someone get away with something "for the sake of the team", or do something else that they know is wrong or may be dangerous. The motivations for these requests are numerous and vary depending on the situation and the people involved. For those who find these requests to be against their ethical standards this can be a hard situation to find themselves in and a difficult decision to make. A decision has to be made however because fence sitting can be just as bad as doing the wrong thing.

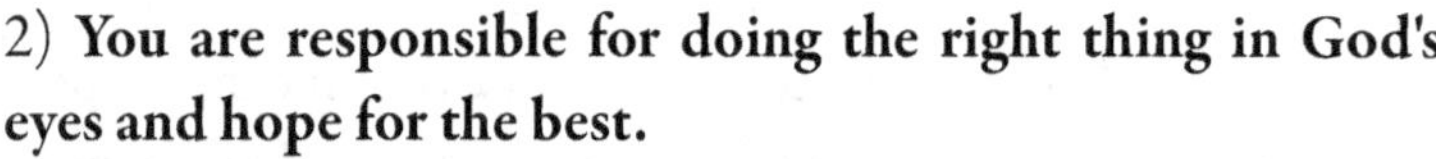

2) **You are responsible for doing the right thing in God's eyes and hope for the best.**

Although we don't have an extensive amount of dialog in the text to tell us what any of the people involved were thinking what we do have says a lot. First of all, although I do not agree with what Pharaoh asked them to do, I can somewhat understand his motivations and his fears. Did that make it right in the eyes of God? No! Shiphrah and Puah could not use the decrees of the king or their fear of his wrath to justify breaking the commandments. They took responsibility even though it displeased their earthly master because they knew who it was more important to please. Could their story have ended badly? Yes. They may have been killed, beaten, or received some other dreaded punishment. They could not have

known for sure how God would help them out but they trusted
that He would and were willing to do what was right regardless
of the consequences. That is why I admire them.

3) Not all blessings are tangible.

At the end of their story, it says that they were blessed
with "houses" which means that their lines would live on. As
family relationships can be eternal they may be surrounded by
many of their descendants in the Spirit world. There is another
important blessing though can be attributed to these women.
Even though we do not know for sure if one or both of them
were there when Moses was born they were probably well
known within the Israelite community. We do not know if
there were other midwives that were working in the
community or not but it is unlikely because they probably
would have been called before Pharaoh as well. Even if they
were not there when he was born, their courageous example
of defiance of the king in order to keep the commandments
of God may have been one of the things that helped Moses'
family find their own courage to hide him and then set him
adrift in the basket allowing him to grow up into one of the
greatest leaders in Israel's history. If this is true then millions
upon millions of people throughout history have benefitted
from their example without even realising it.

Pharaoh's Daughter and Moses' Parents - Making a Legend

This chapter is going to be a bit different because I feel that there is no single star in the story of Moses. No matter how isolated we may feel at times all of us have been shaped into the person we are today and are continuing being shaped into the person we will become by those with whom we associate with. For most people their family can be the most influential people in their lives - in both good and bad ways. Regardless of if your parents are present or absent in your life they will be an example to you.

It is generally an accepted fact that Moses was one of the greatest prophets who ever lived. He is admired by both Jews and Christians alike. Indeed, although all of the revelations he received came from God, they are often referred to as "The Law of Moses" to distinguish them from the writings of all the other great prophets who have lived. Knowing the specific skills that Moses would need to become a great leader God gave him a very special upbringing by allowing him to have two families - his natural family and his adoptive family - both of whom he lived with during different parts of his life.

His story starts off after we have had the scene set in Exodus 1 where Pharaoh had made the decree that all male Israelite children were to be killed at birth. As you know from the previous chapter the Israelite midwives were not following that decree and as a result many male children lived but their lives were still in danger as the text tells us that "... there went a man of the house of Levi, and took *to wife* a daughter of Levi. And the woman conceived, and bare a son: and when she saw him that he *was a* goodly *child,* she hid him three months."[231] Hebrews 11:23 gives us a little more insight into their reasoning because it adds that they "...were not afraid of the king's commandment." Now as many of us who have been around babies know, the older they get the bigger, more active, and louder they get which makes them harder to keep under wraps. This seems to be the case for Moses because his mother is forced to give him up in order to protect him. No mother should be forced to do this.

"And when she could not longer hide him, she took for him an ark of bulrushes, and daubed it with slime and with pitch, and put the child therein; and she laid *it* in the flags by the river's brink. And his sister stood afar off, to wit what would be done to him."[232]

Now when I've read this account in the past I have not thought about what his mother must have been feeling as she did this. I feel guilty now because I've just skimmed over it and, because I knew how the story ended, never thought how hard this must have been for her. Unless she had received revelation from God that everything would be okay she had no way of knowing what would happen to her son once she set him adrift.

True, her daughter stood by watching what was going to happen but she was a child or a teenager at best. If an Egyptian came by and decided to harm him there would have been nothing Miriam could have done to stop them. The ark would protect him from drowning but starvation, dehydration, and being eaten by animals was still a possibility. This brave mother, after putting her own life in danger for three months by hiding her child, showed faith and courage by literally putting the fate of her child into God's hands. She probably walked away with a prayer in her heart and tears in her eyes wondering if she would ever see him again.

Happily, he did not die and the second mother in Moses' life enters the scene.

"And the daughter of Pharaoh came down to wash *herself* at the river; and her maidens walked along by the river's side; and when she saw the ark among the flags, she sent her maid to fetch it. And when she had opened *it,* she saw the child: and, behold, the babe wept. **And she had compassion on him**, and said, This *is one* of the Hebrews' children."[233]

Compassion is "sympathetic feeling: pity, mercy".[234] All of the definitions for compassion apply to Pharaoh's daughter based on what she does next. First off it says that he was crying when she opened the ark. We do not know how long he had been there by now so the poor thing was probably hungry, scared, tired, and/or needed a diaper change. Unless she had a heart of stone she had to feel both sympathy for him and also pity. Her next actions show that she also felt mercy towards him.

"Then said [the baby's] sister to Pharaoh's daughter, Shall I go and call to thee a nurse of the Hebrew women, that she may nurse the child for thee? And Pharaoh's daughter said to her, Go. And the maid went and called the child's mother. And Pharaoh's daughter said unto her, Take this child away, and nurse it for me, and I will give *thee* thy wages. And the woman took the child, and nursed it. And the child grew, and she brought him unto Pharaoh's daughter, and he became her son. And she called his name Moses: and she said, Because I drew him out of the water."[235]

I am going to give Pharaoh's daughter the benefit of the doubt and assume that she was an intelligent woman capable of making rational decisions and solving puzzles. She had already figured out that this was a Hebrew child and, unless Pharaoh had not made his decree known within the palace, could probably figure out that he had been put there because his parents had defied her father by not killing him at birth. Then a Hebrew girl who knows enough about the situation to know that the child would need a nurse approaches her and offers to find one for her. Unless Hebrew children made a habit of hiding in the reeds and approaching Egyptian officials that they did not know this had to be slightly suspicious. Once the nurse is brought she would have been able to tell that it was in fact the child's mother due to her reaction upon seeing her son unless Moses' mother was one heck of an actress. Now Pharaoh's daughter has a decision to make. She can either turn them in and allow her father to make an example of them or she can defy him as well by allowing the child to keep living. She chooses the later and not only shows mercy by allowing the child not only to live but to live with his family until he is old enough to be weaned upon which time she adopts him as her own. While we don't know what all of her motivations were we can infer a few things from this:

1) She may not have completely agreed with her father's decree to kill the male children.

I don't know if the Pharaoh at this time was a tyrant or not. Whether he was or not her decision to let the child live was in direct defiance to him. She had to know that this may have put her own life in danger or at the very least given him cause to become angry with her. Unless she was naturally rebellious she most likely did not have a habit of disobeying her father so this may have been uncharted territory for her and yet she does not appear to hesitate in making a decision.

2) She wanted the child to know his heritage.

Even though she had figured out that the child was a Hebrew, and had apparently decided to adopt it when she first saw him, did not mean that she had to let him know his heritage. Unless there would be no way that people could assume he was an Egyptian she could very well have found an Egyptian woman to nurse the child for her. She was a member of the royal family after all. By letting his mother raise him for the first few years of his life this Egyptian princess was allowing Moses to learn something of the Hebrew culture before becoming her son and being raised as an Egyptian prince. She would have known that his parents would raise him as a Hebrew because they would not have known what life in the Egyptian court was like.

The decisions of both Moses' sets of parent had significant effects on this future leader. For one thing we know that Moses eventually chose Israel over Egypt. He may have lived as an Egyptian for most of his childhood and young adult years but when he became an adult he decided which nation he would be loyal to. The account in Exodus 2 almost makes it sound like he accidentally fell into it because he killed an Egyptian and had to run for his life which is why we are blessed to have a second account in Hebrews 11.

"By faith Moses, when he was come to years, **refused to be called the son of Pharaoh's daughter**; Choosing rather to suffer affliction with the people of God, **than to enjoy the pleasures of sin for a season**; Esteeming the reproach of Christ greater riches than the treasures in Egypt: for he had respect unto the recompence of the reward. **By faith he forsook Egypt, not fearing the wrath of the king**: for he endured, as seeing him who is invisible."[236]

These verses make it clear that Moses not only understood the worldly consequences of denouncing his adopted family but the spiritual ones as well. Through both his sets of parents he was given the knowledge that he needed to make an informed choice. I would imagine that his birth mother helped him start to sow the seeds of his faith in God while his adopted mother educated him at a higher level than he could have had at home. As a prince he would have been raised to be confident and taught leadership skills even though he lacked confidence in his ability to speak. He became a man that God knew He could trust to perform this important assignment and we should be grateful to the two mothers and father(s) in his life for helping him become this man.

UNLIKELY RIGHTEOUSNESS: UNSUNG HEROES OF GENESIS

Lessons from the parents in Moses' story include:

1. A knowledge of what is right is inherent in all of us.

Pharaoh's daughter was an Egyptian and we have nothing to indicate that in general she was sympathetic to the Hebrews. We also don't know how she personally felt about her father's decree to kill the Hebrew children - she may have been sickened by it or simply indifferent to it thinking that it would never affect her personally. Her decision to protect and raise Moses shows that she understood that walking away and letting him die was wrong. Whether this knowledge came from a moral upbringing or was a gift from God doesn't matter. The important thing is that she knew.

2. Courage requires action regardless of the outcome.

As mentioned earlier we have nothing indicating that Moses' parents knew he was going to be safe when his mother left him by the river. They had already shown great courage by not killing their son at birth and hiding him for three months. We know that Moses had at least two siblings (Miriam and Aaron) who were also in danger should he be discovered by the Egyptians upping the stakes in the decision that they had made. We know that both his parents decided to defy Pharaoh and have to assume that they were both involved in the plan of what to do with him after they could no longer hide him. Making the decision to give their son a chance by putting him in an ark shows courage and faith under extremely difficult circumstances. Their sacrifice was rewarded handsomely and their relief must have been great when they saw the outcome of their decisions.

3. We honour our parents through the choices we make.

While it says that Moses deliberately chose his natural family over his adoptive family that does not mean that he forgot the kindness of the woman who helped raise him. Even if by choosing to reject the Egyptians he also chose to reject his adoptive mother the choice he made to follow God honoured her for eternity. This brave woman will forever be tied to him because of the Lord's choice to call him as a prophet. He was a great leader and her role in his story is indisputable.

Epilogue

These people were just like us. They had trials, challenges, weaknesses, and strengths. Some of them succeeded and through their actions taught us the way that we should live. Others were not quite so successful but still had their moments where they made good choices. The one thing that they had in common is that they were important enough to not only have their stories written down but those stories have survived for the thousands of years since their deaths. May you live your life in such a way that centuries from now people will admire you for what you did.

[1] Moses 5:13-16

[2] Note: modern revelation has shown that he wasn't the first-born. See Moses Chapter 5 in the Pearl of Great Price.

[3] Genesis 4:3-5

[4] Moses 5:5-8

[5] Moses 5:18-21

[6] Genesis 4:6-7

[7] Moses 5:22-26, emphasis added

[8] Moses 5:27

[9] Genesis 4:8

[10] Moses 5:29-33

[11] Genesis 4:9

[12] The Church of Jesus Christ of Latter-Day Saints. (2003). "Old Testament Student Manual: Genesis-2 Samuel", Intellectual Reserve, Inc., United States of America, 360 p. Section 4-5, p. 52.

[13] Genesis 3:8-11

[14] Genesis 4: 10-12

[15] Genesis 4: 13-14, emphasis added

[16] Genesis 4:15-16, emphasis added

[17] Mosiah 29:12

[18] Church of Jesus Christ of Latter-Day Saints. (October 2010). *Land of Pharaohs* written by Richard Romney, October 2010 addition of the Liahona. Downloaded on July 5, 2015 from, https://www.lds.org/liahona/1990/10/land-of-the-pharaohs?lang=eng

[19] Genesis 12:10

[20] Genesis 12:11-13

[21] Abraham 2:22-25, emphasis added

[22] Genesis 12:14-16

[23] Dictionary.com. (2015). Downloaded on July 6, 2015, from http://dictionary.reference.com/browse/entreat

[24] Genesis 12:17

[25] Genesis 12:18-19

[26] Genesis 12: 20

[27] Genesis 16:1

[28] Genesis 16:2-3

[29] Doctrine and Covenants 132:34-35

[30] Abraham 2:11

[31] (Church of Jesus Christ of Latter-Day Saints. (1995). *Proclamation on the Family*. Downloaded on August 17, 2015, from http://www.mormonnewsroom.org/article/proclamation-on-the-family)

[32] Genesis 16:4

[33] Merriam-Webster Dictionary, 2004. Page 196.

[34] Genesis 16:5-6

[35] Authors note: at the time of this writing, I have never been pregnant. I have been around enough pregnant women though to know that the changes going on in their bodies can cause all kinds of emotional and physical turmoil. We aren't told how far along she was at this point in the story so it is anyone's guess what kind of symptoms she may have been experiencing. Since this was probably her first pregnancy it all would have been new to her and maybe slightly scary.

[36] Genesis 16:7

[37] Genesis 16:8-9

[38] Genesis 16:10-12

[39] Genesis 16:13, emphasis added

[40] Genesis 16:15-16

[41] Genesis 21:10

[42] Genesis 21:11, emphasis added

[43] Genesis 21:12-13, emphasis added

[44] Genesis 21:14

[45] Genesis 21:15

[46] Genesis 21:16

[47] Genesis 21:17-18

[48] Genesis 21:19-21

[49] John 8:11

[50] Genesis 20:1

[51] Genesis 20:2

[52] Genesis 20:3-7, emphasis added

[53] Genesis 20:8

[54] Genesis 20:9-10, emphasis added

[55] Genesis 20:11-14

[56] Genesis 20:14-15

[57] Genesis 20:16

[58] Merriam-Webster, Incorporated. (1994). *The Merriam Webster Dictionary*. P. 623

[59] Genesis 20:17-18

[60] Genesis 21:22-23, emphasis added

[61] Genesis 21:24-25

[62] Genesis 21:26-32

[63] Genesis 26:6-8, emphasis added

[64] Genesis 26:9-10

[65] Genesis 26:11

[66] Genesis 26:12-15

[67] Genesis 26:16

[68] Genesis 26:26-29, emphasis added

[69] Genesis 26:30-33

[70] Genesis 24:1

[71] Genesis 21:5

[72] Genesis 23:1

[73] Genesis 24:2-4

[74] Genesis 24:5-9, emphasis added

[75] Genesis 24:10-11

[76] Genesis 24:12-14

[77] Genesis 24:15-16, emphasis added

[78] Genesis 24:17, emphasis added

[79] 1 Samuel 16:7b

[80] Genesis 24:18-20

[81] Genesis 24:21-23, emphasis added

[82] Genesis 24:24-25

[83] Genesis 24:26-27

[84] Genesis 24:28

[85] Genesis 24:28

[86] Genesis 24:29

[87] Genesis 24:30-31, emphasis added

[88] Genesis 24:32-33, emphasis added

[89] Genesis 24:33-49

[90] Genesis 24:50-51

[91] Genesis 24:52

[92] Genesis 24:53-54

[93] Genesis 24:55

[94] Genesis 24:56, emphasis added

[95] Genesis 24:57-58

[96] Genesis 24:59-61

[97] Genesis 24:62-67, emphasis added

[98] Genesis 25:21, 26

[99] Genesis 25:22-26

[100] Genesis 26:34-35, 27:46, and 28:1-7

[101] Genesis 29:2-9

[102] Genesis 29:10-12

[103] Genesis 29:13-14

[104] Genesis 29:15

[105] Genesis 29: 16-18

[106] Church of Jesus Christ of Latter-Day Saints. (2003). *Old Testament Student Manual: Genesis-2 Samuel*. Published by Intellectual Reserve, Inc., United States of America, 360 pages. Chapter 7, p. 87.

[107] Genesis 29:19

[108] Genesis 29:20

[109] Genesis 29:21-23

[110] Genesis 29:25

[111] The Merriam Webster Dictionary. (2004). P. 80.

[112] Genesis 29:26-27

[113] Author's note: Some people have argued that Jacob brought this on himself because of his interactions with his brother in Genesis 25:29-34 and deception of his father in Genesis 27:1-30. While this may be true it does not justify the actions of Laban. The text does not indicate that Jacob has been anything but honest with him so far so why he did he do this to him?

[114] Genesis 29:28

[115] Genesis 30:27

[116] Genesis 30:28

[117] Genesis 30:29-30

[118] Genesis 30:31-34

[119] Genesis 30:35-36

[120] Genesis 30:37-43

[121] Genesis 31:1-2

[122] Genesis 31:3-16

[123] Genesis 31:17-18, 20-21

[124] Genesis 31:19

[125] Genesis 31:22-23

[126] Genesis 31:24

[127] Genesis 31:25-28

[128] Genesis 31:29-30, emphasis added

[129] Genesis 31:31-32

[130] Genesis 31:33-35

[131] Genesis 31:36-42

[132] Genesis 31:43-53, emphasis added

[133] Genesis 31:54-55

[134] Genesis 29:16-17

[135] See Mathew 22:23-33, Mark 12:18-27, and Luke 20:27-38

[136] Genesis 29:30

[137] Genesis 29:31-35, emphasis added

[138] See Exodus 2, Exodus 4:14, and Luke 1:5

[139] Mathew 1:1-17

[140] Genesis 30:1-4

[141] Genesis 30:5-8

[142] Genesis 30:9-13

[143] Genesis 30:14-21, emphasis added

[144] Genesis 30:22-25

[145] Genesis 31:4-13

[146] Genesis 31:14-16, emphasis added

[147] Genesis 33:1

[148] See Genesis 34 and Chapter 9 of this book for details.

[149] Genesis 35:16-20

[150] Genesis 35:21

[151] Genesis 35:22

[152] 2 Samuel 6:14-23

[153] Job 2:9-10

[154] Genesis 35:27-29

[155] Genesis 37:1-2

[156] Genesis 37:3-4

[157] Genesis 37:5-11

[158] Genesis 37:12-34

[159] Genesis 49:29-31

[160] Genesis 25:21, emphasis added

[161] Genesis 25:22

[162] Genesis 25:23

[163] Genesis 25:24-27

[164] Genesis 25:28

[165] Genesis 25:29-34, emphasis added

[166] Church of Jesus Christ of Latter-Day Saints. *Old Testament Student Manual Genesis-2 Samuel*, (1980), 82–90. Downloaded on November 29, 2016, from https://www.lds.org/manual/old-testament-student-manual-genesis-2-samuel/genesis-24-36-the-covenant-line-continues-with-isaac-and-jacob?lang=eng&query=esau+birthright

[167] Genesis 27:1-4

[168] Genesis 27:5-10

[169] Genesis 27:11-13

[170] Genesis 27:14-17

[171] Genesis 27:18

[172] Genesis 27:19

[173] Genesis 27:19-23, emphasis added

[174] Genesis 27:24-27

[175] The Church of Jesus Christ of Latter-Day Saints. (2004). *Preach My Gospel: A Guide to Missionary Service*. Chapter 3: Lesson 1: The Restoration, p. 44.

[176] Genesis 27:28-29

[177] Genesis 27:30-31

[178] Genesis 27:32-33, emphasis added

[179] Genesis 27:34, emphasis added

[180] Genesis 27:35-38, emphasis added

[181] Genesis 27:39-40

[182] Genesis 27:41

[183] Genesis 27:42-46

[184] Genesis 28:6-9, emphasis added

[185] Genesis 33:1-3

[186] Genesis 33:4

[187] Genesis 33:5-7

[188] Genesis 32:13-21

[189] Genesis 33:8-11, emphasis added.

[190] Genesis 33:12-16

[191] Genesis 35:27-29

[192] Genesis 36:1-5, 8-43

[193] See Genesis 13

[194] Genesis 36:6-7

[195] Genesis 34:1-2

[196] See Genesis Chapter 20:21

[197] dictionary.com: Defile. Copyright 2015, downloaded on May 16, 2015 from http://dictionary.reference.com/browse/defile?s=t

[198] Genesis 34:3

[199] 2 Samuel 13:1-19

[200] Genesis 34:4-6

[201] Genesis 34:7-12

[202] Genesis 34:13-19, emphasis added

[203] Genesis 34:19

[204] The Merriam-Webster Dictionary. 2004. *Honourable definitions 1-3, 5*, p. 345.

[205] Genesis 41:1-7, emphasis added.

[206] Genesis 41:8

[207] Proverbs 15:22

[208] Genesis 41:9-13

[209] Genesis 41:14

[210] Genesis 41:15

[211] Genesis 41:16, emphasis added

[212] Genesis 41:17-24, emphasis added

[213] Genesis 41:25-32, emphasis added

[214] Genesis 41:33-36

[215] Genesis 41:37-38, emphasis added

[216] Genesis 41:39-45

[217] Genesis 41:46-49, 53-57

[218] Genesis 47:1-2

[219] Genesis 47:3-4

[220] Genesis 47:5-7

[221] Genesis 47:8-10

[222] Exodus 1:6-8

[223] Genesis Chapters 42-46

[224] Genesis 41 and Genesis 47:1-12

[225] Exodus 1:9-14

[226] Genesis 46:34

[227] Exodus 1:15-16

[228] Exodus 1:17, emphasis added

[229] Exodus 1:18-19

[230] Exodus 1:20-21

[231] Exodus 2:1-2

[232] Exodus 2:3-4

[233] Exodus 2:5-6

[234] The Merriam Webster Dictionary. (1994). *Compassion,* p. 163.

[235] Exodus 2:7-10

[236] Hebrews 11:24-27, emphasis added

Don't miss out!

Visit the website below and you can sign up to receive emails whenever Tina Kowalski publishes a new book. There's no charge and no obligation.

https://books2read.com/r/B-A-YRLWB-JUAWD

BOOKS 2 READ

Connecting independent readers to independent writers.

Did you love *Unlikely Righteousness: Unsung Heroes of Genesis*? Then you should read *Awesomely Awkward Dating Tips For Beginners*[1] by Tina Kowalski!

[2]

What if everything you thought was wrong with your dating approach is actually what makes you uniquely lovable? Have you been trying to hide your awkward moments when you should have been highlighting them? Prepare to see your dating 'failures' in a whole new light.

Written by someone who went from being chronically single to finding her perfect match, this book challenges everything you thought you knew about successful dating.

1. https://books2read.com/u/3LBpGN

2. https://books2read.com/u/3LBpGN

Through a collection of hilariously honest stories – from accidentally eating ants on first dates to engagement announcements interrupted by grandmother's loud birth control concerns – the author proves that authentic connections don't require perfect execution. Her journey, supported by the innovative 'Awkwardness Scale,' shows how embracing your natural awkwardness can lead to finding genuine love. The author's transformation from a woman who hadn't been on a real date in years to a happily married partner demonstrates that success in love isn't about being smooth – it's about being real. This isn't just a collection of embarrassing dating stories – it's a roadmap to finding love by being unapologetically yourself. Through practical advice and real-life examples, you'll learn that the key to successful dating isn't minimizing awkward moments, but maximizing their potential for creating genuine connections.

Buy your copy today and unlock the power of authentic dating!

Read more at https://books2read.com/ap/RDLvAo/ Tina-Kowalski.

Also by Tina Kowalski

Life Lessons from the Bible
Unlikely Righteousness: Unsung Heroes of Genesis

Standalone
Awesomely Awkward Dating Tips For Beginners
How to Emotionally Survive Cancer

Watch for more at https://books2read.com/ap/RDLvAo/
Tina-Kowalski.

About the Author

Alberta-based author Tina Kowalski is the author of five books and counting, each of which blend humor, faith, and practical advice to help readers navigate life's awkward moments and find joy in even the most difficult situations.

Born in Winnipeg, Manitoba, Tina holds a B.Sc. in Agroecology and has worked across the breadth of Canada in both municipal and missionary service. Her first book, Unlikely Righteousness, explored the lessons we can learn from scripture's unlikeliest heroes. In Awesomely Awkward Dating Tips for Beginners, she shares achingly-relatable anecdotes about finding true love. In How to Emotionally Survive Cancer, Tina bares her soul to help both patients and their caregivers find the resilience they need to endure the unthinkable—and in Leo and Clark's Cat Tips she gives voice to her furry friends as they provide a pet's perspective on owning humans.

Currently, Tina's working on an anthology interpreting Christ's parables for the modern day—once again offering readers a comforting and insightful approach to navigating life's challenges.

Read more at https://books2read.com/ap/RDLvAo/Tina-Kowalski.